KT-583-020

Photoshop® 6!

I Didn't Know You Could Do That...™

David D. Busch

SYBEX®

San Francisco • Paris • Düsseldorf • Soest • London

Associate Publisher: Cheryl Applewood
Contracts and Licensing Manager: Kristine O'Callaghan
Acquisitions and Developmental Editor: Bonnie Bills
Editor: Kathy Grider-Carlyle
Production Editor: Mae Lum
Technical Editor: Susan Glinert
Electronic Publishing Specialists: Susie Hendrickson, Maureen Forys, Happenstance Type-O-Rama
Book Designers: Franz Baumhackl, Kate Kaminski
Proofreader: Mae Lum
Indexer: Ted Laux
CD Coordinator: Erica Yee
CD Technician: Kevin Ly
Cover Designer: Dan Ziegler
Cover Illustrator/Photographer: PhotoDisc

Library of Congress Card Number: 2001086974

ISBN: 0-7821-2918-8

Manufactured in the United States of America

10 9 8 7 6 5 4 3 2 1

For Cathy, the kids, and the country of Spain, without which this book would have had a lot of empty spaces where the illustrations were supposed to go.

Acknowledgments

I'd like to extend thanks to the folks at Sybex, who willingly (and eagerly) gave us the time needed to incorporate all the new and exciting stuff found in Photoshop 6. Major players include Associate Publisher Cheryl Applewood, Acquisitions and Developmental Editor Bonnie Bills, Production Editor Mae Lum (who doubled as the proofreader), Editor Kathy Grider-Carlyle, Technical Editor Susan Glinert, Ph. D., Permissions and Licensing Specialist Dan Mummert, Cover Designer Dan Ziegler, Electronic Publishing Specialists Susie Hendrickson and Maureen Forys, and CD Specialists Erica Yee and Kevin Ly.

Contents

Introduction

Just when you thought you knew everything there was to know about Photoshop, Adobe comes out with an incredible new version that does the impossible: melds a rich gumbo of new dream features with a lithe, easier-to-use interface! Your Photoshop toolkit now includes powerful vector layers; sophisticated new shape controls; text kerning, leading, and warping features; and productivity-enhancing features like the compact Palette Well. It is truly a major upgrade, bristling with dozens of new capabilities worthy of the most powerful image editor on the planet.

However, you probably don't want to bother with feature-by-feature tutorials. You'd rather know what you can do with Photoshop 6 that's exciting, eye-catching, or very, very cool. Did you know that you can:

- Insert Big Ben as the "tower" of a Spanish castle or create other amazing composites?
- Remove your obnoxious ex-relative from a family reunion photo?
- Turn shoebox rejects into triumphant prizewinning pictures with special effects?
- Change daylight scenes into moody dusk or dawn pictures?
- Make mountains out of foothills?
- Create stunning 3D effects from flat objects?
- Build a distinctive logo with one click?
- Morph images to blend or distort them?
- Create macros to perform amazing transformations?
- Multiply one photo into a "picture package" of 5 x 7, 8 x 10, or wallet-sized pictures?
- Annotate your pictures with captions or sound bites?
- Customize Photoshop's interface and tools so the program works exactly the way you want it to?
- Use your computer's memory better?

- ◆ Create new Layer styles that automatically emboss, stroke, shadow, or perform other magic on anything in a layer?

- ◆ Extract images from their backgrounds?

- ◆ Automatically trim images precisely?

This book focuses on dozens of creative ways to transform ordinary images into eye-catching graphics using easy-to-master features found in this image editor. It cuts right to the heart of all of the most misunderstood—but easily applied—tools in the latest version of Photoshop. It is chock-full of with surprisingly Effective examples, simple to follow techniques, and tricks that serve as jumping-off points to spark your own creativity into action.

Just browsing through the book can lead you to a half-dozen stunning effects you can create in five minutes or less. If you invest a few hours, you'll be able to:

- ◆ Create 3D type with shadows, cutouts, and perspective. Add a metallic sheen or a neon glow. You don't need expensive 3D software to achieve these effects: the same magic can be conjured inside Photoshop.

- ◆ Even if you don't know color correction or gamma correction from brightness-contrast controls, and you think a histogram is a cold remedy, you can utilize Photoshop to bring off-color or dull originals to blazing life, ready for use in Web pages and other applications.

- ◆ Create impressive images from scratch. Even the best photo may need some sort of object created with painting and drawing tools. You don't need to be an artist to turn out professional work. Photoshop even lets you create a cool logo with a single click using the new Layer styles capability!

The impatient, the harried, and those who must use Photoshop in their work (but don't want to make a career of this application) will love this book. You are the people who never read the manuals—unless you have to—but instead ask a colleague who's been there to "just tell me how to do this one thing…." *Photoshop 6! I Didn't Know You Could Do That…* provides you with exactly the sort of information you are looking for. Aimed at intermediate-to-advanced Photoshop users who want to spread their wings and learn more, this book, like the other books in the IDKYCDT series, serves as a light-hearted and fun way to glean cool Photoshop ideas.

Is This Book for Me?

This book is for you if you're a Photoshop 6 user, or if you plan to upgrade soon. Although many of the techniques do work with Photoshop 5.5 and earlier versions, I've given preferential treatment to new features and, where procedures and dialog boxes have changed, describe only the Photoshop 6 version.

This book is for you if you're looking for things you didn't know you could do with Photoshop, and you can do without lengthy discussions of things you already know. There are many computer books with 300 pages of solid information. Unfortunately, they're often 800-page books! Too frequently, all that extra verbiage is expended with unnecessary hand-holding designed to teach absolute beginners how to open files, set basic tool options, and other basic stuff. The step-by-step instructions often list the same obvious procedures, each time they are used, consuming valuable space and wasting your time.

You already know how to duplicate a layer; why should an author tell you to drag the layer to the New Layer icon in the Layers Palette every time you need to produce a new copy? If you don't happen to know that particular Photoshop shortcut, you do know how to find Layer ➢ Duplicate in the menus without a lot of prompting. Once you learn where the Brightness/Contrast controls are, do you really need a step that says "Choose Image ➢ Adjust ➢ Brightness/Contrast"?

So, this book is aimed at graphics workers who already know basic Photoshop functions, and who want only a reminder or shortcut now and then. You want to know the general procedure for producing an effect, how varying parameters in a dialog box change the results of a procedure, and some ideas for applying your own creativity to a technique.

If that describes you, you'll love the no-nonsense, "compressed" step-by-step instructions in this book. A typical step might look like this:

> Create a custom shadow by duplicating the tower layer and then filling it with black (remember to mark the Preserve Transparency box in the Fill dialog box). Then soften the shadow using Gaussian Blur (I used a 7.5-pixel radius in this case), and choose Edit ➢ Transform ➢ Distort to stretch the shadow out realistically on the ground. Reduce the Opacity of the shadow layer so it blends in with the ground.

But don't worry; there will be plenty of reminders, shortcuts, and explanations to help anyone who may be rusty or still developing their Photoshop skills. This book is for you if you're looking for new ideas and are willing to spend the time experimenting to make them work for you.

How This Book Is Organized

This book is divided into nine parts. Each part is a collection of numbered sections that tell you how to do a cool thing with Photoshop.

In "Customize Photoshop," you'll learn how to bend the image editor to your will, maximize your working space, add sticky notes and audio annotations, and avoid one particularly messy Windows 2000 memory pitfall. Some tips on working more efficiently with a graphics tablet are also included.

"Make Eye-Popping Graphics by Combining Images" shows you how to make mountains out of foothills, demonstrates how to move the Eiffel Tower to the seashore, and reveals secrets for using the incredible Extract command. You'll learn photocompositing from a new perspective.

"Retouch Your Images" takes you on a step-by-step tour of traditional photo retouching, including removing age lines, improving the appearance of facial features, and removing dust spots. Other projects show you how to simulate sharpness in blurry images, and use blurriness as a creative tool.

"Correct Your Colors!" shows you how to change moods with color, ways to compensate for weird or off-color lighting, how to fix annoying color casts, and how to make weak colors look richer and more vibrant.

In "Transform Images," you'll learn how to turn a photo into a fine-art painting, add a soft, romantic haze to a portrait, and paint with lighting effects. You'll move beyond Photoshop itself to create effects with third-party tools like Alien Skin's Eye Candy 4000.

"Amazing 3D Effects" lifts you beyond the two-dimensional world to creating 3D objects, adding shadows with a single click, and creating eye-catching 3D text effects.

Amazing text effects are yours in "Warp Your Words and Create Other Text Effects," which shows how to get great metallic looks, eerie backlit text, fire and ice, and bent text using Photoshop 6's new Text Warp feature.

Learn to create great macros and use Photoshop's other automation tools in "Streamline and Supercharge Photoshop." You'll never reinvent the wheel again.

"Work on the Web" takes you on a tour of Photoshop and ImageReady's Web tools. You'll find out how to optimize file size and colors, and how to animate images.

Signposts Along the Way

As is customary with books of this sort, you'll find additional material inserted in the text to help you work better, faster, or more wisely.

NOTE Notes give you ideas for doing things more quickly or for applying a technique in a way you might not have thought of. They can include interesting tidbits that you'll want to absorb and use in your own work. They can also include interesting information that is not essential, but which provides additional insight, background, or explanations of why things work as they do.

WARNING Warnings are important caveats that alert you to pitfalls you may encounter along the way. Ignore them at your own risk. Some apply only to specific platforms or situations, but it's best to be forewarned and forearmed.

The Eternal Battle

As we slog through the twenty-first century, Photoshop and the graphics arena in general remain the last great battlefield in the platform wars between Mac OS and Windows. Although Windows combatants have the numbers in their favor, the Macintosh (along with Photoshop) remains the weapon of choice for a huge number of graphics professionals. Any book written about Photoshop must speak to both camps.

I understand the problems intimately. I bought one of the first Macintosh computers available the week they were introduced in early 1984, and I have followed the upgrade path through Fat Mac, Macintosh II, Quadra, PowerMac, and beyond. I've used IBM PCs even longer, but I had to wait patiently for a decade (or so) until Windows graphics capabilities caught up (so to speak) with that of Mac OS. As a Photoshop worker since version 2, I've dealt with Windows/Mac issues on a daily basis.

So, this book covers Photoshop as it is used on both platforms. In practice, there is not a lot of difference. Except for keyboard shortcuts and some memory issues, Photoshop works identically on both types of machines, with exactly the same tools, options, menus, and dialog boxes. Indeed, the only way you can tell whether a dialog box was extracted from one OS or another is to look at their title bars or note the location of the Close boxes and/or Zoom/Maximize-Minimize boxes.

The figures in these pages were taken from both systems, and I hope you didn't decide whether or not to buy the book based on how many screen shots you counted from your favorite platform. Instead, I trust you'll see that I've covered things like the Mac's special way of handling memory right alongside a potentially crippling bug found in Photoshop when it runs under Windows 2000. This is an equal opportunity book.

The only other thing to be aware of is how I've handled the keyboard/mouse differences issue. Rather than weigh down the text with notes like "press Option+I (or Alt+I if you're using Windows)" I have settled on a series of widely used conventions, as follows:

Alt/Option means to press the Alt key if you have Windows or the Option key if you are using Mac OS.

Ctrl/Command means to press the Ctrl key if you're using Windows or the Command key if you're using Mac OS.

Click means to click the left mouse button if you're using Windows (or the right button if you're left-handed and have reversed the order of the buttons) or simply click if you're using a single-button Macintosh mouse.

Right/Ctrl+click means to click using the right mouse button under Windows (again, unless you're left-handed) or to hold down the Ctrl key and click if you're using Mac OS. Note that the Macintosh has *both* a Command and Ctrl key: the Command key is the equivalent of the Windows Ctrl key, and the Mac Ctrl key is not.

The CD

Admit it. You have half a dozen books in your library with the accompanying CD-ROMs still sealed in plastic. You still haven't found a compelling reason to open them. The CD-ROM bundled with this book will quickly become an old friend and valued tool. That's because you'll find the material on it genuinely useful. The CD icon is used in the text to alert you to tools and resources you'll find on the CD-ROM.

Here's a general description of what you'll get:

◆ Try-out software, plug-ins, and other goodies. Many of the third-party tools mentioned in this book will be found on the CD-ROM in versions for Windows, Macintosh, or both. Check them out. A full list of products can be found in the "About the CD" section at the end of the book.

◆ Full-color versions of all the projects in this book. Sybex pulled out all the stops to include a lush 16-page color insert with this book with many of the best illustrations in color. However, you'll want to examine my original images to see exactly how an effect looks in Photoshop. Every figure and graphic in the book is located on the CD-ROM so you can study it in detail.

◆ Original images and working files. You're free to try out any of the techniques using your own images, of course, and I hope you will. But if you want to follow along using the same images I worked with, you'll find them on the CD-ROM. Separate folders are provided for each chapter, and the files are sorted by project for easy identification.

◆ Clip art. These additional images lend themselves to the projects described in the book. You can use them for your own variations on Photoshop themes.

◆ Miscellaneous stuff. These include actions, and other things from the book that will enhance your Photoshop experience.

Customize Photoshop

The latest version of Photoshop is more customizable than ever. You can adjust how your brushes work, free up some space on your screen by tucking palettes out of the way in the Palette Well, and tell Photoshop to resize windows automatically when you zoom in and out. There are lots of things you can do if you know a few tricks. This is *not* one of those chapters that tell you how to set up all your Photoshop humdrum preferences. I'm going to concentrate on customization steps that even Photoshop veterans sometimes neglect or don't use fully.

Let's face it: Photoshop has a lot of features you need, but you don't need them all at once. Photoshop has ten conventional palettes and a Toolbox palette that can eat up a lot of your screen real estate, leaving less room for you to see and work with your image. Photoshop 6 provides some new features that make it easier to allocate the area on your screen. Here are several ways to maximize your working space.

1 Maximize Your Monitor

One of the fastest ways of increasing your workspace is to maximize how you work with your monitor display. Try these tips:

♦ Get a larger monitor. Serious Photoshop workers probably already have the largest monitor they can justify, and new computer packages have included nothing smaller than 17-inch displays for years. However, unless you're already using a 21- or 22-inch display, you can make some serious improvements to your Photoshop working environment by upgrading to a larger monitor. The "sweet spot" right now contains those compact 19-inch displays that don't take up much more desk space than a 17-inch CRT, yet offer 25 percent more image area. The older, curved-tube 21-inch monitors will eventually be displaced by new flat-screen 22-inch monitors and so-called "wide aspect" displays with 24-inch diagonal measurements, but any of these larger monitors are big, bulky, and expensive compared to 17- and 19-inch options.

◆ Switch to the highest resolution you can work with comfortably with your monitor. At higher resolutions, all of the Photoshop palettes and menus become relatively smaller, giving you more working space. Try a 1024 x 768 setting with a 15-inch monitor; 1280 x 1024 with a 17-inch monitor; or 1600 x 1200 with a 19- to 21-inch monitor. One Sony 24-inch display allows 2304 x 1440 resolution! If the maximum resolution seems too drastic, drop back one setting. I use 1280 x 1024 on my 19-inch monitor. This figure shows Photoshop at (clockwise from upper left) 800 x 600-, 1024 x 768-, and 1280 x 1024-pixel resolutions. Notice that at 800 x 600, there isn't even room for the Palette Well, something that is most useful at lower resolutions!

NOTE If you find the menus under a higher resolution setting slightly difficult to read and you're using Windows, switch to the Large Fonts setting. Right-click your Desktop, choose Properties from the context menu that appears, select the Settings tab, and click the Advanced button. You'll then be able to choose Large Fonts from the drop-down list. You'll gain the increased workspace afforded by the higher resolution setting, but you'll still be able to view your menus easily.

WARNING Some graphics cards provide settings that don't preserve the default proportions, or aspect ratio of your screen when compared to your previous setting. For example, you might find both 1600 x 1024 and 1600 x 1200 available. You may need to adjust the Vertical Size control of your monitor so that squares look like squares again, and other objects aren't stretched out of proportion.

◆ Use multiple monitors. You'll need two graphic cards installed in your system (or a single graphic card that can support two monitors) and a pair of displays. A large conventional display for showing your working image and a smaller one (especially a compact LCD panel) allocated to the toolbars work best. Both Mac OS and Windows support this option directly (the Mac practically forever, and Windows since Windows 98, Windows Me, and Windows 2000). Once you've set up the operating system's control panel, you need not make any changes to Photoshop itself. The following figure shows the Macintosh Monitors Control Panel (from an earlier System 7.5 setup) configured to use two monitors.

```
┌──────────────────────────────────────────┐
│ ▣▦  ══════════ Monitors ══════════        │
├──────────────────────────────────────────┤
│ Settings of selected monitor :      v7.5.1 │
│ ○ Grays :  ┌─────────────┐ ⇧  ┌──────────┐ │
│            │ Black & White│    │ Options... │ │
│ ● Colors : │ 4           │    └──────────┘ │
│            │ 16          │    ┌──────────┐ │
│            │ 256         │    │ Identify  │ │
│            │ Thousands   │ ⇩  └──────────┘ │
│            └─────────────┘                │
│ Changes take effect when Monitors is closed. │
│ ┌──────────────────────────────────────┐ │
│ │                                        │ │
│ │                                        │ │
│ │                  ┌────┐┌────┐          │ │
│ │                  │▓▓▓▓││----│          │ │
│ │                  │▓1▓▓││ 2  │          │ │
│ │                  └────┘└────┘          │ │
│ │                                        │ │
│ └──────────────────────────────────────┘ │
│ ○ Rearrange On Restart   ┌────────────┐  │
│ ● Rearrange On Close     └────────────┘  │
└──────────────────────────────────────────┘
```

2 Arrange Your Palettes and Tools

Another way to increase your workspace is to arrange your palettes and tools intelligently so they don't monopolize your screen's available real estate. Try these techniques:

- ◆ Combine palettes to group the ones you use most often. Drag a palette's tab into another palette group to add it to that group. If the Layers, Channels, and History palettes are the ones you use most often, you might want to group them together.

- ◆ Completely hide palettes you rarely use. Click the palette's Close box (at the right-hand corner of the title bar under Windows, or at the left-hand corner under Mac OS) to remove it from the screen. If you find you aren't using the Styles palette much, hide it until you need it. You can reveal the palette again by selecting it from the Window menu.

- ◆ Minimize a palette so only its title bar shows. Under Windows, double-click the title bar to shrink the palette down to the title bar and the palette's tab. Under Mac OS, double-clicking the title bar makes the tab vanish, as well, so click the Zoom button at the right end of the palette's title bar to keep the tab visible.

- ◆ Move a palette out of the way quickly by Shift+clicking its title bar. It will snap to the nearest screen edge.

- ◆ Use Photoshop 6's sensational new Palette Well to remove your palettes from the main workspace, and tuck them away onto the Options bar. Just drag a palette's tab into the Well. Only its tab will be visible. Click the tab to pop up the palette; it remains visible until you click somewhere else in the workspace or press Escape. The next figure shows some palettes tucked away in the Well, with others in the workspace minimized and maximized.

NOTE You might want some palettes to remain visible at all times. For example, if you are working with a document that includes multiple layers, you probably want the Layers palette to be available for reference. Drag the other palettes to the Well, but leave the Layers palette in your workspace so you can view the layers and their relationships to one another. If you want to monitor information using the Info Palette, or move around an image using the Navigator, leave them in the main workspace as well.

◆ If you change your mind about all your adjustments, you can restore your palettes to their default locations by choosing Reset Palette Locations from the Window menu.

◆ Learn how to temporarily hide the palettes and menus using the following key combinations:

Tab   Shows/Hides floating palettes, toolbar, and Option bar.

Shift+Tab   Shows/Hides floating palettes only.

Alt/Option+W, N   Shows/Hides only the Option bar.

Alt/Option+W,O   Shows/Hides only the toolbar.

F   Toggles between normal mode, hiding title bars only, and hiding both title bars and menus.

3 **Optimize Your Options Bar**

Photoshop's new Options bar is a great addition to your toolkit. Instead of forcing you to switch back and forth between your current tool and the Options palette available with earlier versions of Photoshop, Photoshop allows you to make the Options bar (optionally) visible at all times. The Options bar changes form automatically as you switch tools to display only the options for that tool. You have a few options with the Options bar that you might not have been aware of:

◆ By default, the Options bar is docked at the top of your screen, just below the Menu bar. You can grab the "gripper bar" at the left edge of the docked bar and move the Options bar anywhere on your screen.

◆ Drag the floating Options bar to the bottom of the Photoshop workspace to dock it there.

◆ Double-click the title bar of a floating Options bar, or the gripper bar of a docked Options bar, to collapse it so only the active tool's icon is showing. You can see examples of the Options bar positioned at the bottom of the screen and floating in the following figure.

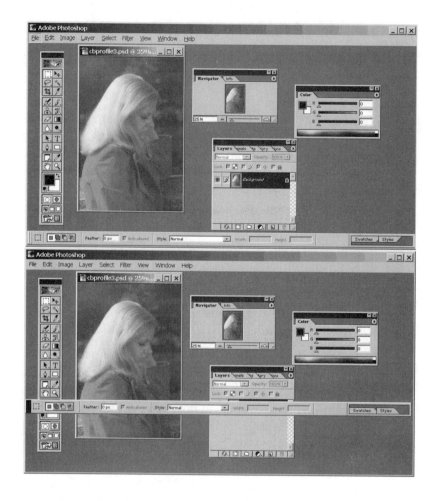

4 Customize Your Canvas Color

Here's something I'll bet you didn't know you could do with Photoshop. The image canvas (the area surrounding your image, not the Photoshop workspace) defaults to a neutral gray. If you'd rather have it be another color, you can do that easily. Just select the color you want for your canvas as Photoshop's foreground color. Then choose the Paint Bucket tool. Hold down the Shift key, and click in the canvas area (you might have to zoom out to make the canvas visible within the borders of the image). The canvas of all open images (as well as any others you open) will display the new color until you switch it to some other one.

To return the canvas to its default color, choose the Colors Palette and type **192** in each of the boxes to the right of the R, G, and B sliders. Then, hold down the Shift key, and click in the canvas area to restore the canvas to its default 25 percent gray value.

5 Make Your Windows Fit Your Image

A surprising number of Photoshop users don't take advantage of the program's ability to resize windows as you zoom. By default, when you zoom in and out of an image, the window containing the image remains the same size, rather than shrinking or growing to match the new zoom level. That's a good thing when you have a small screen (with no extra space to accommodate a growing image), or when you want to tile and view several images at once and don't want one of them to grow and overlap the others as you zoom.

Other times, however, you'd rather have the window grow and shrink as you zoom. Here are two ways to make your image fit better on your screen.

To zoom the image to the largest size that will fit in your workspace without cropping, press **H** to activate the Hand tool, or press **Z** to activate the Zoom tool. Then, you can either click the Fit On Screen button in the Options bar or right/Ctrl-click in the image area and choose Fit On Screen from the context menu that pops up. Note that this procedure can produce *fractional* zoom levels, such as 54.1 percent, if needed, to create an image that fits the workspace completely.

To automatically resize the window so it matches the size of the full image area as you zoom in and out, press **Z** to activate the Zoom tool, and click the Resize Windows To Fit box in the Options bar. The window will change size until it fills the available space on your screen. Then, scroll bars appear so you can scroll to view portions of the image that can't be shown, as you can see in the following figure (which also shows a fractionally zoomed image at left).

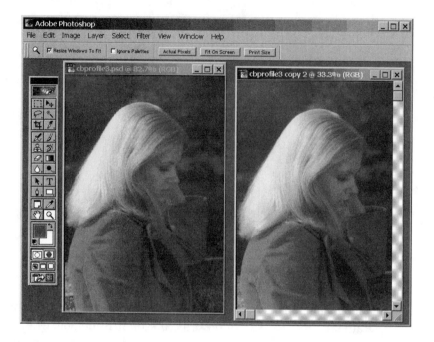

6 **Automatically Update Open Documents**

You're working on a document and decide you need to apply some effects not available within Photoshop. (It's possible!) Say you'd like to use Corel Painter's natural brush tools to add some tasteful brush strokes and then return to Photoshop to perform additional modifications. Wouldn't it be nice to automatically update your Photoshop image whenever you make changes to it using another program(such as ImageReady)? Or, perhaps you're working with a colleague over a network and want to have your copy of an image reflect any changes your co-worker makes. Photoshop can do that with its new automatic update feature. Here's how to use it:

1. Choose Edit ➢ Preferences ➢ General. Mark the Auto-Update Open Documents box, and then click OK to apply the option.

2. Save your image to make the current version available to the other program that will be manipulating it.

3. Make the changes in the other program, and then save to store them to disk.

4. Photoshop automatically updates your image to reflect the changes. If you want to countermand the update, choose Edit ➤ Undo Update From File, or just press Ctrl/Command+Z.

7 Juggle Your Plug-Ins

Here's another commonly known option that not many use to its full capability. Photoshop allows you to specify an additional folder to search other than its own Plug-Ins folder when it loads. There are several situations in which this capability is valuable.

You've got a gazillion plug-ins and want to keep your third-party add-ons separate from Photoshop's native plug-ins. An auxiliary plug-ins directory (not nested within Photoshop's own Plug-Ins folder) can simplify managing those extra filters.

You have a large number of plug-ins that you don't use very often and would prefer not to have them clogging up your Filters menus. (When very large numbers of plug-ins are loaded, Photoshop runs out of room and just dumps the excess into the Other submenu.) Place your rarely used plug-ins in a separate folder, which you can activate or deactivate on a session-by-session basis.

You have some cool plug-ins installed for another application and would like to share them with Photoshop without having to make extra copies in your Photoshop Plug-Ins directory.

Here's how to do it.

1. Choose Edit ➢ Preferences ➢ Plug-Ins & Scratch Disks to produce the dialog box shown next.

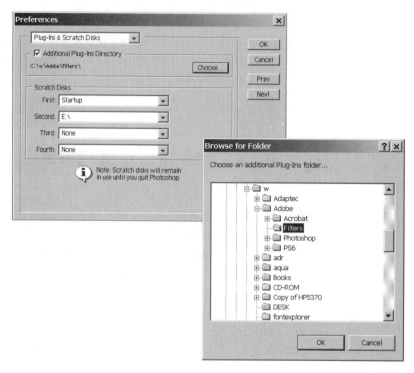

2. Mark the Additional Plug-Ins Directory box, and click the Choose button. Navigate to the folder you want to use, and select it. Click OK.

3. Exit Photoshop, and restart to activate your new option.

4. To temporarily deactivate the extra plug-ins folder, return to the Plug-Ins & Scratch Disks dialog box and uncheck the Additional Plug-Ins Directory box.

NOTE   If you have a plug-in or folder (either in Photoshop's Plug-Ins directory or your extra plug-ins folder) that you'd like to deactivate on a semi-permanent basis, rename it, placing a tilde (~) as the first character of the plug-in or folder name. Photoshop will ignore the plug-in(s) specified, yet you don't have to move or delete them. They'll be there ready for reactivation at any time by removing the tilde from the name.

8 Avoid the Photoshop 6 Memory Trap

Photoshop 6 has a memory bug that can be a killer if you use Windows 2000 and access the Internet regularly. With any luck, it will be fixed by the time this book is published. If not, here's what you can do to protect yourself. Macintosh owners and those using other versions of Windows can ignore this one!

Under Windows 2000, Photoshop 6 can gobble up memory in such a way as to interfere with your Internet access. Without warning, your browser may be unable to locate a particular page, or your e-mail program may be unable to connect with your mail server. This problem plagued me for weeks, even after I figured out it was a memory resources bug. I didn't know the cause. When it hit, I would close programs at random, reboot, and perform mystical incantations over my keyboard. Then I discovered that thousands of Photoshop users shared my problem.

The solution? A bug-fix from Adobe that acknowledges the problem. Unfortunately, at this writing no such bug-fix is available. The workaround is as follows:

1. Choose Edit ➤ Preferences ➤ Memory & Image Cache to produce this dialog box.

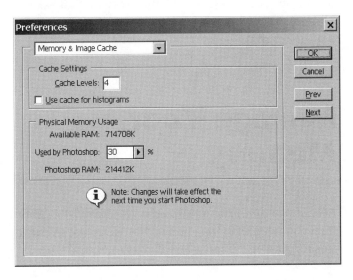

2. In the Physical Memory Usage area, change the Used By Photoshop parameter to 30 percent or less.

3. Click OK to apply the option.

4. Exit Photoshop, and relaunch to activate the new setting, which should solve your initial problem, as it did for me.

Unfortunately, this is one case in which the cure was almost as bad as the disease. Under Photoshop 5.5, I'd been happily editing images with a "mere" 384MB of memory. Because most of what I do involves Photoshop, I set Photoshop memory usage to 80 percent, giving me more than 300MB of RAM for the image editor, and plenty left over for Windows 2000 and other less memory-hungry applications I wanted to run at the same time.

When I changed the usage setting to 30 percent, I noticed a drastic change in how Photoshop worked. With only 100MB or so of RAM, large images, images with lots of layers, and multiple open images quickly consumed all my available memory. Poor Photoshop was forced to use its scratch disks much more often. Performing a simple change to a layer often resulted in a delay as Photoshop wrote information to the hard disk and read back other data it didn't have room for in RAM. What a mess!

I was lucky, however. At the time this happened, memory prices had taken one of their periodic nose-dives and the cost of 256MB modules used by my computer dipped below the $100 mark. I snatched up three of them, upgraded to 768MB of memory, and never looked back. In the new configuration, Photoshop has well over 200MB to work with, even at the 30 percent setting. As a bonus, with all that extra memory not used by Photoshop to work with, Windows 2000 has become a bit more of a speed demon for other tasks.

9 Manage Your Memory

Even if you don't succumb to the Windows 2000/Photoshop 6 memory bug, you need to manage how Photoshop uses your RAM. Here are some tips for getting the most out of your memory.

The obvious: Add as much memory to your system as you can afford (and do it when prices are low!). Photoshop may run on a system with 64MB of RAM, but I've never tried it. Your minimum for Mac OS, Windows 98, or Windows Me should be 128MB of memory. More is even better, as long as you avoid the problems you can encounter if you try to use more than 512MB of RAM with Windows 95/98 or Me. If you edit large images, images with many layers, or have multiple images open at once, expand your memory horizons.

Allocate as much of your available memory as you can to Photoshop. Here's how to do that.

Manage Windows Memory

Windows and Macs manage memory differently. Here's the non-Windows 2000 procedure. (If you're using Windows 2000, read the preceding section about the memory bug.)

1. Within Photoshop, choose Edit ➤ Preferences ➤ Memory & Image Cache.

2. In the Physical Memory Usage area, change the Used By Photoshop parameter. Use a value of 50 to 80 percent, depending on how much memory you have to waste. Allocating more to Photoshop reduces the RAM for other applications, so if you have other programs that need lots of memory, choose a prudent value.

3. Click OK to apply the option.

4. Exit Photoshop, and relaunch to activate the new setting.

Manage Macintosh Memory

Mac OS lets you specify how much memory each application should use. Just follow these steps:

1. If you're using Mac OS 9's Simple Finder, change to the regular Finder. Choose Edit ➤ Preferences, and uncheck the Simple Finder box on the General tab to turn it off.

2. Exit Photoshop. Mac OS can't set memory preferences for an open program.

3. Locate the Photoshop application icon. That shouldn't be hard (I'll bet you find it in the Photoshop folder). However, Mac OS 9's Sherlock 2 can find it for you quickly if you're determined to make technology do the job. Choose Edit ≻ Find to produce the Sherlock dialog box, type **Photoshop** in the Search box, and specify Applications from the drop-down specifications list. Click the Magnifying Glass icon, and Photoshop's location should be magically revealed to you.

4. Select the Photoshop icon, and choose File ≻ Get Info ≻ Memory. You can also press Command+I and choose Memory from the drop-down list in the General Info dialog box. The dialog box looks like this.

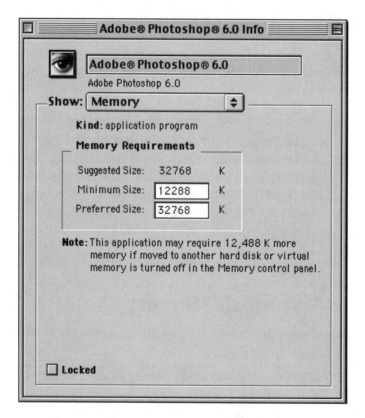

Three different memory values are shown:

◆ *Suggested size* is the value "built-into" the application as a recommendation by the software vendor. (Sometimes this value will be lower than is actually practical, and it was selected because the vendor didn't want buyers to know what an actual memory hog the program is.) You can't change this setting.

◆ *Minimum size* is the amount of memory that's the bare minimum for the application to run. Although some programs do set a minimum that is more than they actually need, Photoshop is not one of them. Leave this setting alone.

◆ *Preferred size* is the amount of memory a program can use if required. It will never use more than this and will, instead, settle for something between the minimum and this size, depending on how much memory is available. You should set this to a large enough value that Photoshop has plenty of RAM to work with, yet there is enough left over for other programs.

You can monitor how much memory Photoshop is actually using by selecting About This Computer from the Finder, and viewing the dialog box shown here.

10 Manage Scratch Disks

Scratch disks are another Photoshop feature that aren't always used to best advantage. Here's how to get the most from your hard disk.

Scratch disks are a kind of private virtual memory used by Photoshop, substituting hard disk space for silicon memory where necessary. Scratch disks are no replacement for physical memory. The difference in speed between magnetic storage and solid state memory is on the order of one second to, say, 32 years (which is what the magnitude is between a millisecond and a nanosecond). However, there are many times when Photoshop will need to resort to disk space.

Photoshop uses your startup disk (the disk used to boot your operating system) as its first scratch disk by default. That may not be your best choice because your startup disk is usually pretty busy handling requests of your Mac's operating system or Windows' own virtual memory scheme (your so-called *swap file* or *paging file*). Ideally, your scratch disk(s) should be a different hard disk and, preferably, the fastest one you have available.

Casual Photoshop users frequently don't have a second hard drive installed. Today's operating systems and computers easily handle large hard disks (even those 80MB and larger) as a single volume, which makes selecting a different scratch disk a moot point. Fortunately, those of us who use Photoshop a lot probably have exhausted the available storage on at least one hard disk and have added a second or third. Here are some tips for choosing a scratch disk that will not slow you down:

◆ Choose a non-startup drive, one that isn't already busy doing non-Photoshop things.

◆ Select your fastest drive. If you're using an external serial drive, choose a Firewire drive over one using the original, slow USB connection. If you have an Ultra-DMA EIDE drive or, better yet, a SCSI drive, use that. While Ultra-DMA disks have transfer rates that rival even the speediest SCSI models, SCSI can still be better because the SCSI bus is designed for multitasking. You'll often get better performance than with an EIDE disk that shares one of the two EIDE channels with other devices.

◆ If you don't have a free hard drive, create a partition on an existing drive and use that as a scratch disk.

◆ Keep your scratch disk defragmented, using your favorite defragmentation utility.

◆ If you have multiple drives, you can specify several of them for use as scratch disks. Choose Edit ➤ Preferences ➤ Plug-Ins & Scratch Disks, and choose the disks using the dialog box that appears next. (The Windows dialog box is similar.)

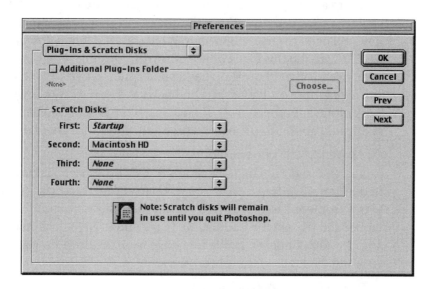

You can monitor how much scratch disk space you have available and how it is being used in the Preview box in the Status bar at the bottom of the screen. Click the right-pointing arrow (➤) next to the Preview box, and choose Scratch Sizes from the menu that pops up. Thereafter, the scratch disk storage used/available will appear in the preview window, as shown below.

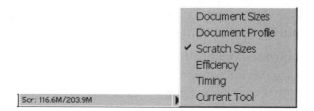

11 Add File Info

One of the biggest problems that a programmer who is maintaining an application is faced with is trying to figure out what various snippets of code are supposed to do. Months or years may have passed since the program was created. Photoshop images can be almost as confusing. You return to an image to make a few changes, but you can't recall how you achieved an effect. Or, perhaps the image was created by someone else and now you must reverse-engineer it. What was that font before it was raster-ized? Where did this logo come from? What was this image used for? The good news is that Photoshop has a good collection of tools that can help you avoid these problems. The bad news is that nobody knows how they work or never bothers to use them. Here's the first of a collection of note-taking and annotation tools you probably never thought of using.

Choose File ➤ File Info to produce the File Info dialog box. What in the heck is that, you say? Prepare to be amazed. This little-used dialog box has no fewer than *six* different pages, all ready to accept tons of information that you, or someone else, may find useful later. This is all stuff that can be embedded right in the Photoshop image and used to decipher an image after the fact. Choose the File Info page from the drop-down Section list. Here are the kinds of things you can add:

Caption   There's space to write a caption used when the image is published, added to a DTP layout, or otherwise distributed. You can enter the name of the person who created the caption (in case you need to check facts later on), place a suggested headline, and embed special instructions for using the photo.

Keywords   Type a keyword into the box provided, and click Add to enter a new, searchable keyword for categorizing the image. Some image cataloging programs used by professional news organizations can search Photoshop files for these keywords.

Categories   Enter an alphabetic category code of three characters. These categories are defined by professional news organizations, and they probably are not needed by Photoshop users who don't work with them.

Credits   Enter the correct credit information for a copyrighted image, such as photographer and source information.

Origin   Used to provide information on the history of the image. The Object Name field contains a short identification, date, and location.

Copyright & URL   Used to enter additional copyright information or a URL if information about an image can be found on a Web site.

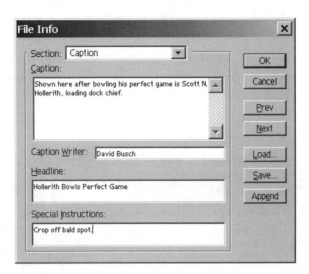

NOTE You can add File Info to Photoshop (PSD) files, as well as TIF, JPEG, EPS, and PDF formats under Microsoft Windows. If you're using Mac OS, you can add File Info to any file format.

12 Add a Sticky Note

You can plaster sticky notes all over your image, too, using the Photoshop Notes feature. You can hide or edit the notes, reposition them, and color code them for quick reference. Here's how.

1. Press **N** to activate the Notes tool, and choose Notes if the Audio tool is active.

2. Click in the image where you'd like to paste the note. For example, you might want to insert a note saying how an image should be retouched or leave instructions on what needs to be done next.

3. In the Options bar, enter an author for the note (if different from the default user of this copy of Photoshop), and choose a font and font size (graded from smallest to largest, rather than a fixed point size).

4. Choose a color for the note from the Options bar. You can use different colors to further differentiate between authors or to indicate urgency (green, yellow, red, etc.).

5. Resize the note window if desired, as shown in this figure.

6. Enter the text for your note.

7. When you are finished, click the note's Close box in its title bar to reduce the note to an icon.

8. You can drag and position the icon anywhere you want in the document.

Here are some of the things you can do with these notes:

◆ Show or hide the notes by choosing View ➢ Show ➢ Annotations.

◆ Expand a note from an icon by double-clicking it.

◆ Edit a note by expanding it and revising the text.

◆ Delete a note by selecting it and pressing Delete.

◆ Remove all notes by right/Ctrl-clicking any note and choosing Delete All Annotations from the context menu that pops up. You can also select a note, and click Clear All in the Options bar.

◆ Move a note's icon by dragging it (the note will still pop up in its original location, however).

◆ Relocate a note's window by opening the note and dragging its title bar to the new location.

13 Add a Sound Bite

If a microphone is connected to your computer, you can add audio notes, as well. These are great for adding annotations that would take a long time to type, or are better explained through voice notes. Just follow these steps:

1. Press **N** to activate the Notes tool, and choose Audio if the Notes tool is active.

2. Enter options in the Options bar, such as the author.

3. Click in the image where you'd like to include the audio annotation. The dialog box shown next pops up.

4. Click the Start button (Windows) or Record (Mac OS), and begin speaking into the microphone.

5. Click Stop when finished.

N O T E If you're using Mac OS, the dialog box looks like this. You can pause and re-sume recording, and monitor the length of your annotation.

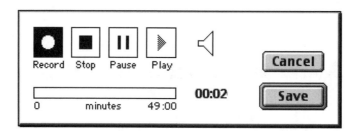

6. To play the audio annotation, double-click its icon.

N O T E One sometimes-overlooked way of annotating your images is to give the layers descriptive names, rather than default to Photoshop's Layer 1, Layer 2, Copy of Layer 1, etc. nomenclature. Prior to Photoshop 6 you could rename a layer by double-clicking the layer in the Layers palette and entering the new name. With Photoshop 6 and later versions, this still works with the Background layer. However, if you double-click any other layer, the Layer Styles dialog box appears. If all you want to do is rename a layer, hold down the Alt/Option key as you double-click the layer.

14 Apply Grays Under Pressure (and Colors, Too)

Can you sign your name with a bar of soap? Can you sign it with a cue ball? How about with a pen? When it comes to anything more precise than signing your name (such as sketching or outlining a selection), a clunky mouse or a loose-cannon trackball is outshined by a pressure-sensitive tablet every time. If you're serious about graphic work with Photoshop and have any artistic ability at all, you must add a tablet to your repertoire.

The advantage of a tablet and cordless pen is that you can draw lines precisely, varying the thickness of the lines or the opacity of the colors you're using simply by pressing down harder. That lets you work as though you were using a real-world tool like a pencil, so you can achieve more subtle effects. Make a mistake? Just flip the stylus over and use its "eraser" end. You can set the tablet to respond to changes in pressure by varying the size of the brush, its opacity, and its color. Best of all, you can set your preferences for how you want the pen to respond by *tool*. In Photoshop, you can use a pressure-sensitive pen with the Magnetic Lasso, Magnetic Pen, Pencil, Paintbrush, Airbrush, Eraser, Clone Stamp, Pattern Stamp, History Brush, Art History Brush, Smudge, Blur, Sharpen, Dodge, Burn, and Sponge tools.

Pen tablets also include productivity enhancing features, such as programmable menu strips that let you summon frequently used commands with a click of the pen. The stylus can double as a mouse for selecting menu items, tools, or dialog box options, or you can use a regular mouse (including special models furnished with some tablets) in tandem. Wacom's pens include a switch button that rocks forward and back, and they can be programmed to deliver your favorite keystrokes or clicks, depending on how you press the switch.

I opted for a compact Wacom Intuos model with a 6 by 8-inch active surface that occupies the same area on my desk as my mouse pad. A smaller 4 by 5 model is available for what I'd consider casual use, and there are other versions up to a mammoth 12 by 18-inch tablet. Here's how to choose the right tablet for your work:

- ◆ Choose a small tablet (in the 4 by 5 or 6 by 8-inch range) if you want to be able to sketch quickly or outline a selection. However, if your working area is large, a small tablet can be clumsy to use.

- ◆ Select a larger tablet (in the 12 by 12 or 12 by 18-inch range) if you need to work with full-page layouts, want to trace images (just slip the original under the tablet's transparent overlay), or are doing animation. The extra size lets you work precisely even on a grand scale.

Photoshop 6 lets you set your pressure-sensitive pen's options for each tool using a dialog box like this one.

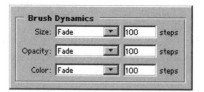

You can turn any of the three parameters (Size, Opacity, and Color) on or off separately, so you can use them individually or in combination. You can also set the number of steps the pen will apply between the lightest pressure and the heaviest. A small number (say, 10 steps) means the pen will modify the parameter (such as size) in 10 increments between the largest pen size (light pressure) and the smallest (full pressure). So, you can make your effects as subtle as you like. This figure shows a brush stroke that was set to vary only in size (at the top), in opacity (second from the top), in color (you can't see it in black and white, but the stroke changes from black to red), and (at the bottom) with all three parameters specified.

The following figure shows one application for a pressure-sensitive stylus. I used the pen with Photoshop 6's new Liquefy tool to blur a busy background.

Make Eye-Popping Graphics by Combining Images

It would be nice if every image contained every element you wanted, in exactly the right place. However, there's a lot you can do to remedy imperfect arrangements with Photoshop. You can easily combine images, move parts of images from one place to another, and perform other magic to create an idealized or fantasy image from a collage of pieces. Whether you want to make mountains out of foothills, or move the Eiffel Tower to the seashore, Photoshop has the tools you need.

Combining images can be a complex task, so I'm going to break the process down into easy steps with a series of projects that use an expanding roster of techniques. All of the images used in this chapter are provided on the CD-ROM accompanying this book, so you can work along with me if you like.

15 Move the Eiffel Tower to the Seashore

One of the simplest tasks facing anyone who wants to combine images is the chore of extracting a component from one picture and inserting it into another in a realistic fashion. This exercise may not be particularly realistic (although transplanting the Eiffel Tower to the Atlantic coast is a charming idea); however, it will show you what to do.

1. Start with a photo of the Eiffel Tower, and select only the tower itself. Because the sky is dreary and contrasts nicely with *la Tour Eiffel,* the simplest way to select it is to use the Magic Wand tool. Set the Tolerance to 32 in the Options bar, and click several times in the sky area until most of the sky is selected, as you can see in this figure.

NOTE A sneaky way of experimenting with Tolerance levels when making selections of this sort is to toggle in and out of Quick Mask mode by pressing **Q**. The selected area will appear as red (assuming you have Quick Mask Options set to show the selected area as red), so you can easily see how much of the desired pixel area is chosen. Switch back, and change to a different Tolerance level to select fewer or more pixels without grabbing pixels in the area you don't want to select.

2. Choose Select ➢ Similar to grab pixels similar to those in the sky area you have selected. This will capture the sky area that shows between the framework of the tower.

3. Press Shift+Ctrl/Command+I to invert the selection so only the Eiffel Tower is selected. Then copy the image so you can paste it down in our seashore vista.

4. Paste the tower in a suitable location in the oceanfront picture, as you can see in this figure.

5. The picture actually looks pretty good as-is, but you might want to add some other features to provide a more realistic look, based on how the original image was illuminated. For example, if the picture was taken late in the afternoon, you might want a shadow. Or, you might want to include a reflection in the water. I've done both here.

◆ Make the reflection by duplicating the tower, inverting it, and blending it in with the background. I applied Photoshop's Soft Light blending mode to the reflection layer to soften it and merge smoothly with the water layer underneath.

◆ Create a custom shadow by duplicating the tower layer and then filling it with black (remember to mark the Preserve Transparency box in the Fill dialog box). Soften the shadow using Gaussian Blur (I used a 7.5-pixel radius in this case) and choose Edit ➢ Transform ➢ Distort to stretch the shadow out realistically on the ground.

16 Make Mountains Out of Foothills

If you can't get to the mountain, bring the mountain to you. Sometimes you can improve a scenic photo simply by adding a few things that weren't there in the first place. I started with this photo of a rolling valley nestled between the foothills of a mountain range. You can see a few snow-capped mountains at the horizon, but the image could benefit from some drama.

1. Switch to the picture of the flat plains with the mountains in the distance, as shown next. Select the mountains and sky using the Rectangular Marquee.

2. Switch back to the rolling valley picture, and select the sky area using the Magic Wand, as you did in the previous project. Press Delete to cut the sky pixels from the image.

NOTE If you get rough edges in the sky gap you create, use the Magic Wand to select the area again and use Select ➤ Modify ➤ Expand (with a 1-pixel setting), followed by Delete to smooth the area.

3. Paste the snow-capped mountains and cloudy sky you copied from the plains picture into a new layer, and move the layer under the valley layer so the new sky shows through. Resize the mountains/sky so they fill the gap above the rolling valley.

4. Select the valley layer, and use Layer ➤ Layer Style ➤ Outer Glow to apply a fuzzy halo around the valley. The key dialog box settings can be seen in the following figure.

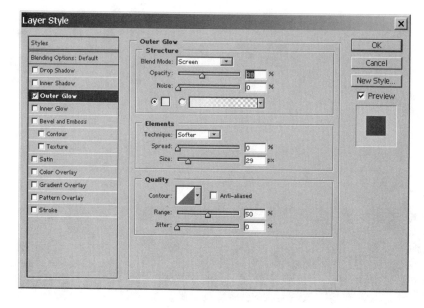

◆ Set Opacity in the Structure area to about 38 percent. The glow is intended to simulate a faint fog that's barely visible behind the foothills.

◆ Also in the Structure area, make sure the default Foreground-To-Transparent gradient is selected from the drop-down list, and choose a very light whitish-blue as the foreground color. That combination provides a realistic fog look.

◆ In the Elements area, choose Softer, and move the Size slider to about 29 pixels.

NOTE When combining images, you don't necessarily want the elements to blend smoothly together. Instead, you'll often want *separation* between the elements. The easiest way to do that is with a subtle Outer Glow halo (to separate dark objects), a drop shadow (good for separating lighter objects), or even a duplicate of the top object, which provides harder edges than the object alone.

5. Use Image ➢ Adjust ➢ Levels to make sure that all the available tones in the sky are within the boundaries of the dark and white points. In the dialog box shown next, I've moved the left, black-point slider to the right until it matches the beginning "foothills" of the Input

Levels histogram. Then, I moved the right, white-point slider to the left to the point where the white tones began to fall off. Adjust the middle gray slider until the range of tones looks best.

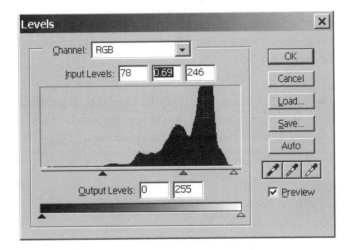

6. Use Filter ➢ Render ➢ Lens Flare to add some realistic sun glare to "finish" the image. (We're not quite done with this scene yet, so let's move on to the next project.)

17   Add a Castle in Spain

It's fairly simple to merge soft-edged elements like mountains and clouds. Things get a little trickier when you attempt to combine substantial pieces like, say, a castle.

1. Using the castle picture on the CD-ROM, select the sky using the Magic Wand, invert the selection, and copy the castle and its surrounding hillside to a transparent layer, as shown here.

2. Using the picture of the rocky gorge, select the river area and invert the selection so only the rocky slope is selected. Copy it to a transparent layer, and resize to form a foundation for the castle.

3. Position the rocks beneath the base of the castle and use the Eraser tool and a soft brush to blend the two. Merge the two layers, copy, and paste into the image you created in the previous project.

4. Add a soft Outer Glow Layer style to the castle to provide some separation with the background.

5. Darken the bottom of the rocky base. Then flatten the image. You should end up with a graphic that looks something like the following figure.

18 Extract an Object with the Magnetic Lasso

If an object has well-defined edges, Photoshop's Magnetic Lasso tool is often the best way to select it. The Magnetic Lasso attempts to cling to the edge (an area of high contrast) of the image, so you can quickly drag a selection border. I used it to extract an image of a car from its background. Follow these steps to learn some tips for using this tool:

1. Choose the Magnetic Lasso from the toolbox. If necessary, press the Caps Lock key to change the cursor to a circle with a crosshair in the center.

N O T E   If you have set the cursor for Other Tools to Standard in the **Display & Cursors** Preferences dialog box, the Magnetic Lasso cursor appears as a Lasso icon unless you turn on Caps Lock. If you've set the cursor for Other Tools to the Precise setting, the Magnetic Lasso cursor displays as a circle with a crosshair no matter what your **Caps Lock** state.

2. Move the crosshair to an edge in the image at a point where you'd like to start drawing the selection. Click once. You do not need to hold down the mouse button.

3. Drag along the edge of the object. Click at any point when you're satisfied with the selection line to "lock in" the line to that point, as shown in the following figure. The click action lays down an anchor point. Note that Photoshop inserts an anchor point at intervals even if you don't click.

4. If the Magnetic Lasso isn't grabbing the edge correctly at a certain point, hold down the Alt/Option key to revert to the standard Lasso tool. Release the key when you want to return to the magnetic version.

5. As you drag the selection, you can back up to the previous anchor point at any time to redraw the magnetic line. If you want to retreat past an anchor point, press Delete to remove the last point.

N O T E   Photoshop examines the area inside the cursor circle to decide where the edge is. You can reduce or enlarge the cursor "brush" using the same technique you use to switch to the next larger or smaller brush when painting with Photoshop: the left bracket ([) key makes the circle/brush smaller, and the right bracket (]) key makes it larger. The width, in pixels, is reflected in the Options bar as you enlarge or shrink the cursor.

6. When you've finished making the selection, either click at the point where you started, double-click the mouse button, or press Return/Enter.

Here are some tips for getting the most from the Magnetic Lasso:

◆ Use the Edge Contrast control in the Option bar to determine how sensitive the Magnetic Lasso is. Choose a low-contrast setting (lower than the 10 percent default value) if the edge is not distinct. Use a high-contrast setting if the edges are clearly defined.

◆ Don't be afraid to touch up parts of the selection that aren't perfect. Use Quick Mask mode to erase or add to the selection. You can also use the standard Lasso, holding down the Shift or Alt/Option keys to add or subtract from the selection. You can also click the Add To Selection and Subtract From Selection buttons in the Options bar if you'll be doing a lot of adding or subtracting to avoid having to hold down a key.

◆ Make the Magnetic Lasso more sensitive by adjusting the frequency of the anchor points it lays down automatically. A high number (up to 100) will increase the number of anchor points created as you drag. A low number decreases the number of points. If you enter **0** in the Option bar, Photoshop will not create any anchor points at all until you click the mouse.

◆ Your graphics tablet really shines with this tool. Mark the Stylus Pressure box in the Option bar, and Photoshop will vary the size of the cursor's sensitive area based on how hard you press down on the stylus. Press hard to reduce the size of the cursor/brush, and release pressure to make it larger.

7. When you've finished selecting the car, copy it to a transparent layer, as shown in the figure that follows. The exercise that follows this one will show you how to merge it with a suitable image.

19 Match Lighting when Merging Objects

As you might guess, you can't simply drop an object into an image and expect it to look realistic. One key to combining images successfully is to match the lighting and texture of the scene and the object. This project demonstrates some of the tricks you can use to match lighting.

1. Open the file containing the road image from the CD-ROM.

2. Drop the car image onto the road, as you can see in this figure. It doesn't look quite right, does it? That's because the lighting and shadows don't match. The road has shadows cast by the trees, and the car is brightly lit with no shadows.

3. Use the Brightness/Contrast control to reduce the overall contrast of the car image and make it darker, as if it were in shadow.

4. Use the Burn toning tool with a large, soft brush, and darken the front grill and fender area of the car. This is the area that is deepest in shadow.

5. Press **Q** to enter Quick Mask mode, and paint a selection across the hood of the car, as a continuation of the bright stripe of ground that runs horizontal, just behind the front tire. Press **Q** when you are finished to exit Quick Mask mode.

6. Use the Brightness/Contrast control to lighten the area of the hood, as if the bright light were illuminating that section of the car.

7. Press Ctrl+D to deselect everything, and then press **Q** to enter Quick Mask mode again. This time, paint a shadow up the side of the car, corresponding to the shadow that runs horizontally, even with the rear tire of the car. Press **Q** to exit Quick Mask mode.

8. If you like, use Filter ➤ Render ➤ Lens Flare to add a "sunlight" reflection to the rear quarter-window of the car. Your finished image should look like the following figure. Compare it with the one before to see how much more realistic the merger is.

20 Delete Unwanted Areas with the Background Eraser

Another tool that can be used to remove unwanted areas around sharp-edged images is the Background Eraser. This tool has a circular brushlike cursor with a crosshair, just like the Magnetic Lasso. In this case, Photoshop examines the image area under the crosshair and deletes everything within the circle that is similar to the pixels the cursor rests on. Here, we're going to use it to remove the background around a pumpkin, shown in the following figure.

1. Choose the Background Eraser from the toolbox, and select a large, soft-edged brush that will let you paint near the edges of the pumpkin. I used the 35-pixel brush.

2. Because the background we're erasing has a range of colors, set the Tolerance level in the Option bar to about 12 percent. That tells Photoshop to erase pixels that are plus or minus 12 percent of the value of the pixel under the cursor.

3. Choose Find Edges from the Limits drop-down list on the Option bar. This keeps the Background Eraser from creating a faded edge. Use this setting when working with a crisp-edged object like our pumpkin.

N O T E   If the object is not hard-edged, use the Contiguous setting to tell the eraser to delete only areas that touch each other, or use the Discontiguous setting to delete the background between areas (such as tree branches or leaves) that extend out into the background.

4. Set Sampling to Continuous on the Option bar, so the Background Eraser will continue to look at areas under the cursor when deciding what to delete. Use this setting when the background pixels are similar, but not identical. If the pixels are very similar, you can use the Background Swatch setting instead (use the Eyedropper and Alt/Option+click in the background to sample it), as shown in the following figure. This mode has few advantages over simply using the Magic Wand.

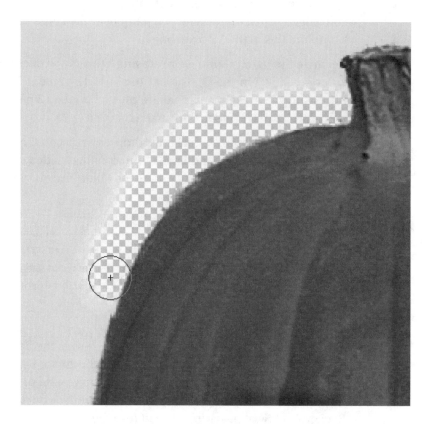

5. Click in your image with the Background Eraser, making sure the crosshair rests on the background and not on the edge of the object you want to keep. Drag the eraser, clicking again each time the background changes to resample. If the background varies quite a bit, you'll want to reclick fairly often. If not, you can drag smoothly to delete pixels.

NOTE Mark the Protect Foreground Color in the Option bar if you want to specify a color that will not be erased. Then, Alt/Option+click the edge of the object at intervals to make that color Photoshop's protected foreground hue.

6. As you drag, you'll erase the background image, and end up with an extracted pumpkin, as shown in the bottom figure.

21 Match Texture and Color when Merging Objects

Lighting isn't the only thing you need to match when combining images. The object you insert should have a color that blends in with the other objects in the image, and its texture should match, as well. Here's some practice at achieving those goals.

1. Extract the rock from the image on the CD-ROM accompanying this book, using one of the techniques discussed so far in this chapter (the Magnetic Eraser is a good choice).

2. Paste it into the elephant image, which is also found on the CD-ROM. I put it in the upper-left edge of the image.

3. Use the Burn toning tool to darken the left edge of the rock to make it conform better to the lighting already in the scene.

4. Next, use Filter ➢ Blur ➢ Gaussian Blur to soften the texture of the rock. Because it's in the background, we might expect it to be slightly out of focus, similar to the trees and other background objects. The image will look like the next figure.

5. Use Image ➢ Adjust ➢ Color Balance, and move the sliders so the rock matches the color balance of the rest of the photo.

NOTE You'll find information on how to balance colors in "Correcting Color," later in this book.

6. Paste the pumpkin image you extracted in the previous exercise, and resize it so it can sit comfortably to the right of the elephant.

7. Switch to Quick Mask mode by pressing **Q,** and paint the "back" surface of the pumpkin to create a shadowed side. Press **Q** again to exit Quick Mask mode.

8. Use the Brightness/Contrast control to darken the shadowed side.

9. Duplicate the pumpkin, and fill it with black. Place this layer below the original pumpkin's layer.

NOTE Actually, it's quicker to leave the duplicate in place and work with the original (which will appear as the layer below it), but some Photoshop neophytes find this confusing. Use whichever procedure is most comfortable for you. One way to avoid the confusion is to immediately rename the duplicate and original layers so they reflect their functions in the image. For example, you could rename the duplicate (upper layer) as Pumpkin and the original (lower layer) as Pumpkin Shadow.

10. Rotate the pumpkin shadow counterclockwise until it's at an angle that duplicates that of the elephant's own shadow.

11. Use Edit ➤ Transform ➤ Distort to stretch the shadow into an elongated form.

12. Set the Opacity of the shadow layer to about 60 percent to duplicate the transparency of the elephant's shadow.

13. Use Filter ➤ Blur ➤ Gaussian Blur, and move the slider very carefully until the edges of the shadow duplicate those of the elephant's.

14. The texture of the pumpkin doesn't match the rest of the photo. Use Filter ➤ Noise ➤ Add Noise, and move the Amount slider to add some monochromatic Gaussian noise. I used a 1.55 percent setting.

15. Flatten the image, which should look something like this.

22 Grab an Image with the Extract Command

Photoshop's Extract command offers the automatic masking tools of third-party programs such as Extensis Mask Pro and Corel KnockOut in an integrated, easy-to-use tool. Extract is your best choice for grabbing objects with wispy edges, such as hair or fur, but it also works with hard-edged shapes. This tool has a lot of options, but you don't need to use all of them to get good results.

Masking is the term for an overlay or layer used to protect portions of an image from modification. It derives from the photographic realm, in which actual film masks were created and sandwiched with an original to produce certain effects, such as sharpening or knocking out the background around an image. In Photoshop, masks are put to a variety of uses, from making selections (for example, with Quick Mask) or modifying how portions of images are combined or blended (as with Layer Masks).

NOTE Photographic masks are created in a variety of ways. Sometimes they are cut from translucent film overlays of rubylith or amberlith. Other times masks are created in the camera using a technique called (naturally) *in-camera masking. Unsharp masking* is performed using a third procedure in which a blurred reversed duplicate of an original image is produced and then combined with it to emphasize the edges. Photoshop can duplicate all three of these techniques right in your computer!

To grab an image, follow these steps:

1. First, select an image suitable for extraction. Images with plain backgrounds work best. (For clarity's sake, I've selected the one shown in the following figure for this exercise.)

N O T E   It's often a good idea to duplicate a layer and use the Extract command on the duplicate. Then, if necessary, you can clone pixels from the original layer if you have erased some portions of the image and want to restore it. You can also use the History Brush to restore erased areas.

2. Activate the Extract dialog box by pressing Alt/Option+Ctrl/Command+X, or choosing Image ➢ Extract from the menu bar. The dialog box looks like the following figure.

3. Zoom in on a portion of the image to begin extraction. You can zoom in exactly the same way as within Photoshop proper: use the Zoom tool on the Extract dialog box's own toolbox, or simply press Ctrl/ Command+space to zoom in or Alt/Option+space to zoom out.

4. Click the edge highlighter or marker tool at the top of the dialog box's toolbox. Choose a brush size that will let you "paint" the edges of the object. I used a 17-pixel brush, selected from the Tool Options area at the right side of the dialog box.

NOTE   If your original image contains a lot of green, you can change the highlight color to another hue in the Tool Options area of the dialog box.

5. Paint the edges with the marker. Use the Eraser tool to remove markings you don't want. The Hand tool can be used to slide the image area around inside the preview window so you can access additional regions without changing your zoom setting.

NOTE You can click a point, then Shift+click farther along the edge to quickly paint the boundaries of the selection. Press Ctrl/Command+Z to undo the highlight you've drawn since the last time you clicked.

6. When you're finished completely enclosing the object, click the Paint Bucket tool in the dialog box's toolbox and fill the area you want to protect with the fill color. Be sure to enclose the entire area you want preserved, or the fill paint will spill out into the rest of your image! (Photoshop's defaults for the marker and fill color are green and blue, respectively, but you can change these to contrast better with the colors of your image if you wish.) The following figure shows a masked image.

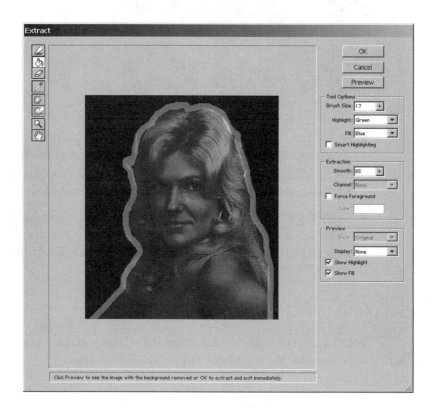

7. Click the Preview button to get a look at what your object will look like when extracted. Photoshop 6 added two new tools to the Extract command to make it easier to fine-tune your extraction.

◆ The Cleanup tool subtracts opacity (or adds it when the Alt/Option key is held down). For example, some area of the hair in the sample picture was made too transparent: when the image was merged with a background, some background showed through. I held down the Alt/Option key and restored some of the area removed by the original extraction command, as you can see in the figure that follows.

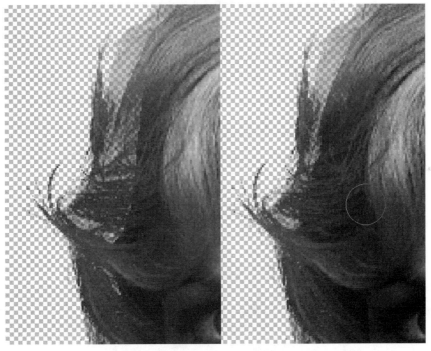

◆ The Edge Touchup tool can be used to sharpen edges that may have become too wispy. Reverse the actions of the Cleanup and Edge Touchup tools by pressing Ctrl/Command+Z.

8. When you're satisfied with the selection preview, click OK to apply the extracted image.

Here are some tips for using the Extract commands's controls:

◆ Adjust the brush width on the fly, using the left and right bracket controls to enlarge or reduce the brush size one pixel at a time. Try to paint over only the minimum area of the original, confining the highlighting as much as possible to the background you want to delete. The size of the brush determines how much of the edge of the object fades; hard edges call for small brushes, mushy edges can benefit from large brushes.

◆ The Preview is shown against Photoshop's traditional gray checkerboard pattern. You will probably get a better idea of what the object will look like when merged with another image by choosing the Black Matte or White Matte backgrounds from the drop-down display list in the Preview area of the dialog box. You can also show or hide the highlighting and fill used to create the preview by marking or unmarking the Show Highlight or Show Fill boxes in the preview area.

◆ If you prefer to end up with a selection, work on a duplicate of the layer. After extracting, Ctrl/Command+click the extracted layer in the Layers palette to convert the extracted image to a selection. You can then save the selection for reuse.

Your finished extracted object should look like the following figure.

23 Add a Background to an Extracted Object

Because the edges of an image grabbed using the Extract command are slightly transparent, you can merge the object successfully with a variety of backgrounds. Let's try out a few.

1. Create a transparent layer under the image extracted in the last exercise.

2. Choose the Gradient tool, and select the Foreground/Background linear gradient. Use a tone and a medium tone as the foreground and background colors.

3. Drag the cursor from the upper-left corner to the lower-right corner. Then, use Filter ➢ Noise ➢ Add Noise to add 10 to 20 percent monochrome Gaussian noise.

NOTE Here's a trick that pros use to improve the look of blended colors and gradients when they are printed. Believe it or not, a smooth transition of colors reproduces more accurately and with less "banding" when a little noise is added. The noise interrupts the gradient enough to make it easier to reproduce, but the noise won't really be visible within the mass of halftone dots.

4. Add an Outer Glow Layer style to provide some separation with the background. The image should look like the following figure.

5. Substitute another background, such as the rustic wood shown at the left in the following figure, or the weathered bricks shown at the right.

24 **Defringe Rough Edges**

When you select an image and paste it down, you'll frequently end up with a fringe of pixels from the background. Photoshop offers at least four ways to eliminate those pixels: the Black Matte, White Matte, and Defringe commands, plus a quick manual method that's superior to any of the other three. You can try all of them using your own image or the portrait I worked with.

1. Using an image that has a plain background, apply the Magic Wand until you've selected most of the background. Press Shift+Ctrl/ Command+I to invert the selection.

2. Copy the selected object, and paste it down into a new, transparent layer.

3. Create a layer underneath the object and fill with black (if the background was light) or white (if the background was dark). This will make the stray white or black pixels around the edges of the object show up better. The image will look like the one in the next figure.

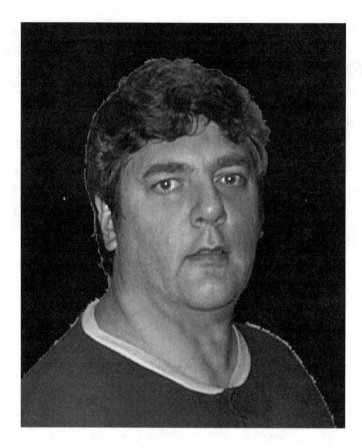

4. Use one of Photoshop's automated tools to try to remove the fringe:

- ◆ Apply Layer ➤ Matting ➤ Remove Black Matte if the object was captured from a dark background, leaving dark-colored fringe pixels around the edges.

- ◆ Apply Layer ➤ Matting ➤ Remove White Matte if the object was captured from a light background (as with this example), leaving light-colored fringe pixels around the edges.

- ◆ Apply Layer ➤ Matting ➤ Defringe. When the Defringe dialog box pops up, enter the number of pixels you think the fringe encompasses. Instead of removing pixels, Photoshop replaces the fringe pixels with pixels sampled from the area around the fringe.

None of these methods produce ideal results. You'll probably get better results using the technique described in the following steps.

1. Choose Select ➤ Load Selection, and choose Layer Transparency from the Load Selection dialog box.

2. Choose Select ➤ Modify ➤ Expand, and enter a small value, say **2** pixels, for the amount the selection should grow.

3. If your pixel fringe is relatively rough, choose Select ➤ Modify ➤ Smooth and enter **2** pixels to smooth it out a bit. Or, you can choose Select ➤ Modify ➤ Feather and enter **2** pixels to blur the edge.

4. Press Delete to remove the selected pixels. The image should look like the one in the following figure.

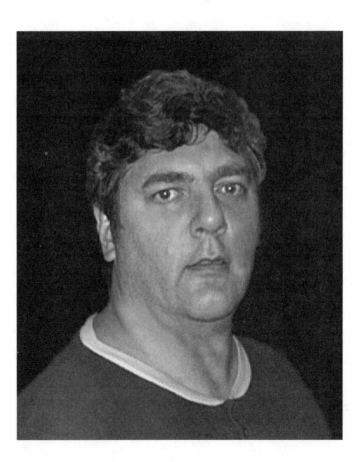

Retouch Your Images

Photo-retouching has come a long way since the advent of the digital age. When I started as a photographer, professional retouching was almost solely within the purview of skilled retouching artists, who worked directly with a print, or the original or duplicate negative or transparency. Brushes and air-brushes, dyes and tints were all tools used to perform image-reworking magic. Today, the photographer or anyone else with a copy of Photoshop can make much the same kinds of modifications faster and more easily.

However, it's useful to keep in mind the artistic heritage of retouching. Perhaps 10 percent of retouching is applying some tone to an image, or cloning an area with the Rubber Stamp. The other 90 percent is knowing *where* to retouch, *what* tone to apply, and exactly *how* to clone. The more experience you have, the better your results will be. So, this chapter provides some practice in retouching images. You learned how to combine images in the last chapter, "Make Eye-Popping Graphics by Combining Images." In the next chapter, "Correct Your Colors!," you'll see how to fix the hues. Taken together, these three chapters give you a good start toward learning how to transform shoebox rejects into triumphant prizewinners.

Retouching is a complex process, so I'm going to work with several images and perform a series of modifications to each, starting with the image of a woman wearing a hat and turtleneck sweater, shown in the previous figure.

There are quite a few defects in this photo (which is why it was chosen). The contrast is wrong. The model's facial expression is not the best. There are some dust spots on the scanned image. A few premature age lines (I think you'll agree any wrinkles before age 60 are premature!) and some slight, but noticeable bags under the model's eyes detract from the picture. We'll fix them one at a time.

25 Erase Double Catchlights

One of the most common errors nonprofessionals make when working with photos is not being aware of the *catchlights* in human eyes. They are caused by reflections of the light source (such as a window, lamp, or the photographer's flash) off the cornea of the eye. We come to expect to see such catchlights because they show that the surface of the eye is moist and reflective and not "dry" and dead-looking. Don't believe me? Compare the two images in the next figure. The one at the right has had the catchlights removed. Unless you saw the two side by side, you'd be hard-pressed to know what was "wrong" with the right-hand photo, but it would look a little spooky to you.

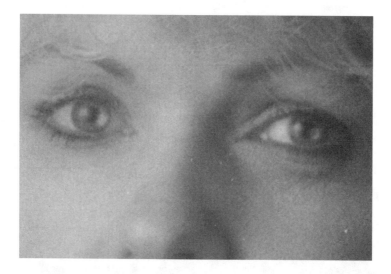

WARNING You can mess with a picture of a scenic landscape, or a building, or almost any object quite a bit before it will look "wrong." However, it's easy to unintentionally distort a picture of a human so the person no longer looks "natural." The eyes, mouth, nose, and skin coloring (in roughly that order) should be given special attention. Make any of those features too large or small, or modify the color even a little bit toward the blue or green range, and you'll end up with an unpleasant portrait.

Our sample image has two catchlights, which came about because the portrait was taken in a studio with a main light off to the left and a second, softer and dimmer light source at the camera position to provide fill light in the shadows. Although the overall lighting is OK, the double catchlights, shown in the next figure, are not.

To remove them, follow these steps:

1. Choose the Burn toning tool from the toolbox.

2. Choose a medium-sized soft-edged brush from the Options bar. In my case, I used the 27-pixel brush, which is slightly smaller than the area to be darkened.

3. Choose Highlights from the Range drop-down list on the Options bar so your darkening will be applied to the catchlight.

4. Set a low exposure ratio so the darkening will happen gradually. About 15 to 20 percent is the most you'll want to use.

5. Paint the right-hand catchlight in each eye with the Burn tool until it darkens to match the rest of the eye surrounding it. Your final image should look like the following figure.

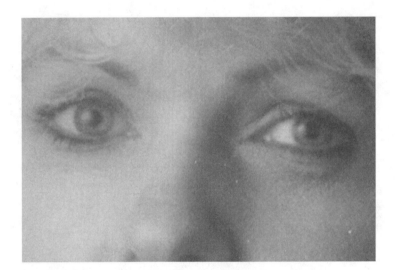

26 Shut Your Mouth

Ordinarily, it's not a good idea to transplant facial features from one image to another. You're better off taking multiple shots and looking for the one with the best smile, most attractive eyes, or most flattering pose. However, that's not always possible. For this project, we're going to cover up the slightly nervous-looking lips in the initial picture with a more subtle, Mona Lisa smile from an entirely different photo. Why? Because we can. And because you might need to.

We're going to extract the mouth from this picture, which has problems of its own. Its defects range from too-tight cropping (the following figure shows virtually the entire film frame) to an emphasis on the wrong set of earrings. However, there's a trace of a smile on the lips that would look good in our original photo.

Follow these steps to perform the transplant:

1. Select the mouth in the donor picture, using the Lasso tool. It's a good idea to grab some of the nose, to use as a reference when resizing the transplanted object.

2. Paste the mouth into the recipient photo, and adjust the new layer's opacity to about 70 percent so you can see the old face underneath the transplanted mouth/nose. That will make resizing easier.

3. Use Edit ≻ Transform ≻ Rotate to rotate the mouth to an angle similar to the one in the original picture.

4. Use Edit ≻ Transform ≻ Scale to resize the mouth so it matches the face, as in the following figure.

WARNING If you'd like fuller lips, you can make the mouth a tiny bit larger, but be very careful. Drastically altering this facial feature will make the photo no longer resemble the original subject. Refrain from this sort of enhancement, unless the person in the portrait is planning on collagen injections of their own!

5. Return the Opacity level of the pasted layer to 100 percent.

6. Use Image ➢ Adjust ➢ Levels or use Image ➢ Adjust ➢ Brightness/ Contrast to match the tones of the pasted image to the original.

7. Use Image ➢ Adjust ➢ Color Balance to correct the color of the pasted image so that it also matches the original. You can make the lips a little redder than they were, if you like.

8. Use the Eraser tool with a large, soft-edged brush to remove everything (but the lips themselves) you pasted. Your image should look like the following figure.

27 Add Some Hair

The model's hair at the left side of the picture isn't quite the way we want it, so we can graft some wispy strands from the same photo that provided the smiling mouth. While we're at it, let's adjust the contrast of the image, too. Get started with the image you ended up with in the previous project.

1. This particular image doesn't require fancy footwork with the Levels or Curves controls. Choose Image ➢ Adjust ➢ Brightness/Contrast, and then reduce the brightness by 20 percent, while increasing the contrast by the same amount. Click OK to apply the modification, and your image should look something like the next figure.

2. Next, return to the "donor" picture we used in the last project, and select the hair at the left side of the face. Again, select some of the eye to simplify resizing.

3. Paste the hair into the recipient photo, and adjust the new layer's opacity to about 70 percent, as you did before, so you can see both the original image and the pasted hair.

4. Use Edit ➤ Transform ➤ Rotate to rotate the hair to an angle similar to the one in the original picture.

5. Use Edit ➤ Transform ➤ Scale to resize the hair so it matches the hair in the original.

6. Use the Extract command, as you learned in the previous chapter, to isolate the hair from its background, as shown in the following figures.

7. Reduce the Opacity of the original image to about 80 percent, so you can move the extracted hair into position more accurately, as shown in the following figure. When you're satisfied, increase the original image's opacity back to 100 percent.

28 Banish Those Blemishes

The final changes we'll make to the image probably won't reproduce well in black-and-white, so you'll want to check out the originals on the CD-ROM accompanying this book to see how dramatic the modifications really are up close and in full color. It's time to put some finishing touches on the picture by retouching out a few dust spots and blemishes. Just follow these steps:

1. Remove the dust spots on the image with the Clone Stamp tool. Press **S** to choose the tool, and select a small, soft-edged brush from the Options bar. Make sure the Aligned box is checked.

2. Hold down the Alt/Option key, and grab a sample of the image close to the dust spot. Then click on the spot to copy some of the image on top of the spot.

NOTE A stylus works especially well for cloning if you have one. Choose Stylus from the Brush dynamics drop-down lists, and set the Opacity to about 40 percent. Then, use the stylus to carefully clone over the dust spots.

3. Use the Clone Stamp tool to erase the bags under the subject's eyes and eliminate any stray hairs that might fall over her eyes. You can see the results of this retouching at the right in the figure below.

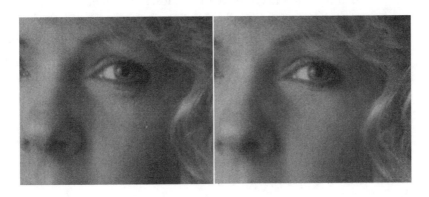

4. Soften any wrinkles around the nose and mouth. You don't want to eliminate them entirely (as you would with cloning); you just want to change some creases into laugh lines, so to speak. Use the Blur tool with a large, soft-edged brush. Set the blur pressure to about 50 percent, and gently smudge away the wrinkles. De-wrinkle the chin and forehead if prudent.

5. Create a new, transparent layer. Choose a color for the model's eyes (I used blue, mostly because the model would break my arm if I gave her green eyes). With a soft-edged brush, paint the irises of the eyes on the transparent layer.

6. Set the eye-color layer's mode to Overlay, and then adjust the Opacity of the layer until the eyes become the color you want.

N O T E   You'll learn more about this colorizing technique in the next chapter.

7. The next few steps can be tricky for guys. You're going to apply some make-up to the model to brighten her look. Women are born knowing this stuff (my 11-year-old daughter can't wait until she's old enough to try out her skills), but males have to learn the hard way. Start out by creating a new transparent layer as you did in Step 5.

8. Select a color for eye shadow. We're in the twenty-first century now, so don't overdo it. (I selected a very faint blue.) Then, paint on the eye shadow, change the mode to Overlay as before, and adjust the Opacity so the eye-shadow is very faint.

9. If you want to enhance the lashes, select them using Quick Mask mode and a fine soft-edged brush to paint a selection on the lashes. Then use Filter ➤ Sharpen ➤ Unsharp Mask to sharpen them up a little.

10. Create another transparent layer, set its mode for Overlay, apply some blush to the model's cheeks, and then reduce the Opacity of the layer until the blush blends in. Your image will start to look like the following figure.

Check out the color original on the CD-ROM to see what's really going on.

11. For some semi-final touches, select the earrings and use the Unsharp Mask tool to sharpen them up. Select the hat, if necessary, and use the brightness and contrast controls to make it a little more visible. Your image will now look like the next figure.

12. I made two more changes to the image. First, I applied Filter ➤ Distort ➤ Diffuse Glow to the image, using a graininess setting of 4, a relatively low glow amount of 4, and a clear amount of 15. This diffuses the image slightly, giving it a romantic look.

13. Finally, I entered Quick Mask mode and painted around the face with a soft brush, so the outer edges of the hair were not brushed. After exiting Quick Mask, I inverted the selection, and chose Image ➤ Adjust ➤ Brightness/Contrast, moved the brightness slider about 10 percent to the right, producing a little more luster in the wispy tips of the hair and the top edge of the hat. The final image looks like the following figure (and please, please check out the full-color version in the color insert and on the CD-ROM).

29 Delete Your Brother-in-Law

Do you remember those photos taken at your wedding reception, in which your new brother-in-law managed to intrude on every photo? Do you have a great-looking group shot of everybody in your department at work—including Elmo, who was fired last month? Wouldn't it be great if you could just paint the offenders out of a photograph with one stroke? Photoshop takes more than one stroke, but it can do the job for you. Try this project to see how easy it is. Lacking a nasty in-law, we're going to clean up a vacation photo by deleting a poorly posed subject, shown at the right in the following figure. Our weapon of choice for this exercise is the Clone Stamp tool.

The obvious solution, of course, would be to crop the kid out of the picture. However, that would snip out the interesting house on the hill in the background. Another remedy would be to copy the portion of the fence at the right of the picture and paste it down over the unwanted subject. Unfortunately, that stretch of fence and its background is very dark, and duplicating it would provide an unattractive dark area at the lower-right corner of the picture. Cloning lets us preserve the background area that's already there, deleting only the boy. Here's how to do it:

1. Press **S** to choose the Clone Stamp tool, and select a medium-sized (say, 35-pixel) soft-edged brush.

2. Hold down the Alt/Option key, and click the foliage between the fence railings to select that area as the source for cloning.

3. Carefully clone over the boy, a little bit at a time. Resample the foliage by Alt/Option-clicking frequently. If your clone "source" (represented by a crosshair that appears briefly to one side of your Brush icon each time you click) moves into an area that has already been cloned, you'll get a repeating fish-scale effect like the one in the following figure.

4. Continue cloning to paint over the boy completely. Don't worry about the fence railing at this time; we'll fix that later. The important thing is to reproduce a realistic background as it would appear behind the subject if he weren't there. After a while, your image should begin to look like the examples shown in the next figure.

5. Copy a horizontal section of the railing from the right side of the fence, using the Rectangular Marquee tool. You should be able to use this tool to select only the fence railing and none of the background area.

6. Paste the horizontal section into the image over a portion of the rail that has been obscured by cloning.

7. Repeat Steps 5 and 6 until all the horizontal railings have been "patched." Then do the same for the vertical railings. Merge all the transparent layers containing the railings. (Make all the layers—except those containing railings—visible, and with the top rail layer selected, press Shift+Ctrl/Command+E. You'll end up with an image that looks like this figure. (I've left the selection boundaries visible so you can see the duplicated portion of the fence.)

8. The remaining boy is still a bit too much taller than the girls in the photo, so you can copy him, paste his image into the picture, and move him down a bit. Use the Clone Stamp tool, as necessary, to blend in the background.

9. Finally, use the Burn toning tool to darken the background and the girls at the left. The finished picture looks like the following figure.

30 Add a Sharper Image

It never fails. You manage to grab the shot of a lifetime and, in your haste to snap, you neglect to focus the camera carefully. Your image turns out blurry! What can you do? Again, it's Photoshop to the rescue.

Parts of an image look blurry when there is little or no contrast between details. You've probably heard this before, and take it as a matter of faith, but I'm going to show you irrefutable evidence. Examine the following figure closely.

The image in the upper-left corner is blurry. The version immediately below it is sharp. Yet you can see from the enlargements at the right that both contain exactly the same number of pixels. The sharp one doesn't have a higher "resolution" than the blurred image. The only difference is that the sharper one has more contrast, specifically at the boundaries or edges between adjacent areas of the picture. To sharpen a blurry image, Photoshop has only to identify the edges and increase the contrast there the most. Let's work with a sample image to see what we can do.

NOTE If you boost the overall contrast of an entire image, it can look sharper, but it won't look as sharp as if you increased the contrast only between the edges.

1. Load the image of the woman and pigeon from the CD into Photoshop. This one needs sharpening only in the foreground, so the first step is to enter Quick Mask mode (press **Q**), and paint with a soft-edged brush to select the face, coat, and hands. Press **Q** again to exit Quick Mask mode to work with your selection, as shown in the next figure.

2. Use the Brightness/Contrast controls to darken the selection and bump up the contrast, as shown in the following figure. That alone will make the adjusted area appear a little sharper.

3. Next, choose Filter ≻ Sharpen ≻ Unsharp Mask, and set the Amount slider to about 150 percent, the Radius slider to 2.0 pixels, and the Threshold value to 2.

Now that you know that sharpening works best when performed on edge pixels, you can understand the options of the Unsharp Masking dialog box better. The Radius slider determines how many pixels adjacent to the edge pixels are used to determine how much the contrast is increased. When this value is set to 0, only the edge pixels are sharpened. With a setting of 2, pixels in a 5-pixel range (the edge pixel and the two closest to the edge) are sharpened. If you're working with a higher-resolution image, you'll want to increase this value even more.

The Threshold slider helps Photoshop determine where an edge is, by specifying the level of contrast that must exist between pixels before they are considered part of an edge. Photoshop looks at the brightness level of adjacent pixels, which are values from 0 (black) to white (255) and then increases the contrast between them (brightening one and darkening the other), depending on whether their original difference passes the threshold you've specified. Set to a value of 0, Photoshop pretends that all pixels are part of an edge and increases the contrast between all of them. With a value of, say, 2, Photoshop will "find" an edge whenever the original brightness value differences are greater than that. With very high settings, Photoshop won't locate many edges and won't do much sharpening.

4. Click OK when you're satisfied with the sharpness, and then repeat the process on the pigeon.

5. That particular day in *le Jardin des Tuileries* was overcast, so I added a little red to banish an overall cyan cast. The final picture is shown below.

31 Make Blur Work for You

It's not the blur that hurts you, it's where the blur is located that can make or break a picture. An action picture with a little blurriness can have a ton more excitement than a razor-sharp stop-action shot in which everyone appears to be petrified by an evil villain's freeze gun. A little judicious blur can also serve to focus interest on the important subject matter of your photograph, while de-emphasizing the nonessential picture elements. This project will show you how to do both. We'll start with the interesting, but not particularly compelling photo shown below.

1. The soccer ball looks like it has been nailed to the ground. Use the Elliptical Marquee tool to copy it, and paste it down in a layer of its own.

2. Now, use the Clone Stamp tool to replicate the grass areas over the original position of the soccer ball, leveling the playing field, so to speak, as shown in this figure. Don't worry about how well you disguise your digital divot, because the grass is going to be blurred in a later step.

3. Drag the image of the soccer ball on the transparent layer up off the ground so it's about at knee-level, as if it had been recently kicked. Then, choose Filter ➢ Blur ➢ Motion Blur. In the dialog box that appears, choose an angle of about –7 degrees and a blur distance of 10 pixels. Click OK to apply the blur.

4. To end up with a shadow of the ball, duplicate the soccer ball's layer, fill it with black (with the Preserve Transparency box marked in the Fill dialog box), and blur it using the same Motion Blur settings as above.

5. Choose Image ➤ Transform ➤ Distort, and stretch the shadow into a more elongated shadow-shape. Set its layer's Opacity to about 50 percent, so it will blend with the grass below. Move the shadow to the left of, and below the ball, to account for the sun's position low in the sky and to the right of the players. Your image will look like this figure.

6. Now, press **Q** to enter Quick Mask mode, and use a large, soft-edged brush to paint a mask on the area surrounding the players. It's OK to have the selection spill over onto the players' arms, legs, and head, if it's only a few pixels. The picture will look more realistic if they are a little blurred, too.

7. Press **Q** to exit Quick Mask mode, and apply Motion Blur to the background, using an angle of 0 degrees and a blur distance of 25 pixels. The final image will look like the one below, and it will approximate what you'd get if a photographer panned the camera from left to right to follow the action. The stationary background is very blurry, and the players, who were moving in the same direction as the camera, are sharper. The faster-moving ball is a little blurrier than they are.

32 Change a Background or Foreground

If a foreground or background area forms a pattern, you can often copy a section of it and paste that over an unwanted object, without the need to tediously clone the area on top of the part being removed. You can use this technique to retouch images of unspoiled scenic areas that aren't as unspoiled as they used to be. Test your skills using this image.

Hundreds of years ago, when the pictured windmills were in active use, workers reached them using the worn trails in the earth you can see about a third of the way over from the right. The demands of tourism prompted the building of the modern paved road seen just left of center. That road is great for getting tour busses to the top of the hill, but it is not very attractive in the photograph. We can get rid of it easily.

1. Use the Lasso tool to select the left hillside area up to the roadside, and copy it to the Clipboard.

2. Paste the hillside duplicate onto a transparent layer, and then move it over to the right so it obscures the road.

3. Use the Eraser tool with a soft brush to blend the edges of the hillside with the rest of the image. You might want to reduce the Opacity of the hillside to about 50 percent, so you can see where the margins of the underlying image are.

4. If necessary, use the Clone Stamp tool to extend the hillside to other areas around its periphery.

5. Flatten the image, and crop the picture to arrive at a final image like the one shown next.

33 Use Blurring and Sharpness as Special Effects

You can retouch photos using blur and sharpening creatively as special effects of their own. Here's a project I came up with to simulate an old "fifties-style" postcard look. To appreciate the contrasting looks and pastel colors, you'll want to check out the original on the CD-ROM accompanying this book.

1. Start with the original photograph shown here. Use the Magic Wand tool to select the sky. Shift-click multiple times in the sky, and use Select ➤ Similar as necessary to grab the whole thing. The contrast between the sky and landscape is high enough that this is an easy step.

2. Save the selection so you can use it later.

3. Make a duplicate of the background layer, and use Image ➤ Extract to grab the tree into a transparent layer of its own.

4. Apply the Unsharp Mask filter to the tree. I set the Amount to 170 percent, the Radius to 2.0 pixels, and the Threshold to 7 levels to provide an exaggerated sharpening, as shown in the following figure.

5. Load the sky selection you made earlier, and apply a Gaussian blur to the sky only. I used a radius of 5.0 pixels to provide a pronounced blurring.

6. Use Image ➤ Adjust ➤ Color Balance, and shift the color of the sky a bit toward the red.

7. Flatten the image, and you'll end up with a picture that looks like the next one. The ultra-sharp tree and foreground combined with the blurry sky give this a fifties, hand-colored look.

Correct Your Colors!

Wouldn't it be great if every image you worked with had perfect color? Wouldn't that save you a lot of time twiddling with hues in Photoshop? Guess again. Because our color perception and taste are highly subjective, there is no such thing as perfect color. If you were framing a picture for display in your home, you might prefer to see a Fall landscape in delicate pastels to better harmonize with a room's muted décor. A graphic artist preparing a brochure to promote tourism might shoot for vibrant, fully saturated colors that would create the urge to jump in your car and visit before those vivid leaves fall from the trees.

Or you might want to add a bluish cast and darken an image drastically to simulate a moonlit night. Perhaps, your sunset photo isn't quite the dusky red you want. An image that looks great on your computer screen probably won't seem quite as overwhelming as an ink-jet print. In short, perfect color isn't a fixed, immutable thing: it's the color that achieves the particular look you're striving to achieve.

I'm going to show you at least four different ways to change the color balance of an image—each easier than the last. You'll find you can make some perfectly wretched images look great—if you know what to do.

NOTE The black-and-white illustrations in the main body of this text obviously don't illustrate color correction concepts very well. You'll want to check out the full-color illustrations in the color insert or, preferably, view all the color figures on the CD-ROM accompanying this book.

34 What's Wrong with This Picture?

The first step to optimizing color is deciding what it is you don't like. It's a bit like creating a sculpture by starting with a chunk of marble and hacking away everything that doesn't look like your subject. To perfect the color in your image, you need to decide whether the color balance is off (and in what direction), whether the saturation of the colors needs to be changed, how light or dark the image should be, and what the contrast between light and dark areas should be. All of these must be considered in terms of your final destination, such as video screen, printer, or printed page. Alter the factors that detract from your image for its intended destination, and you should end up with "ideal" color.

NOTE *Color balance* is the relationship between the colors used to produce your image. In Photoshop, these are most often red, green, and blue, unless you're working with some other color model, such as CMYK (cyan, magenta, yellow, black). *Saturation* is the richness of the colors; red, for example, can range from a pale pink to a glowing crimson. *Lightness/darkness* is the overall brightness of an image. *Contrast* is the range and number of steps of individual tones between the lightest and darkest.

Before using any of the color correction techniques that follow, examine your image, keeping these factors in mind. Here's a quick checklist that might help you get started:

1. First, decide whether the image has an undesirable color cast. That is, in RGB mode, how much red, green, and blue are in your image? If you have too much red, the image will appear too red. If you have too much green, it will look too green. Extra blue will make an image look as if it were created under a full moon at midnight at the North Pole. Other color casts are produced by too much of two of the primary colors, when compared to the remaining hue. That is, too much red and green produce a yellowish cast; red and blue tilt things toward magenta, and blue and green create a cyan bias.

2. Next, examine the color saturation of your image. Saturation is determined by how much of the hue is composed of the pure color itself, and how much is diluted by a neutral color, such as white or black. Think of a can of red paint and white paint. Pure red paint is fully saturated. As you add white paint, the color becomes less saturated, until you reach various tints of pink. Color can also become desaturated by adding black paint, making it darker. Photoshop can help you adjust the saturation of a color by removing these neutral white or black components.

3. Evaluate the brightness and contrast of the image. Brightness and contrast refer to the relative lightness/darkness of each color channel and the number of different tones available. If, say, there are only 12 different red tones in an image, ranging from very light to very dark, with only a few tones in-between, then the red portion of the image can be said to have a high contrast. The brightness is determined by whether the available tones are clustered at the denser or lighter areas of the image. Pros use some things called *histograms* to represent these relationships, but you don't need to bother with those for now.

This figure illustrates these relationships.

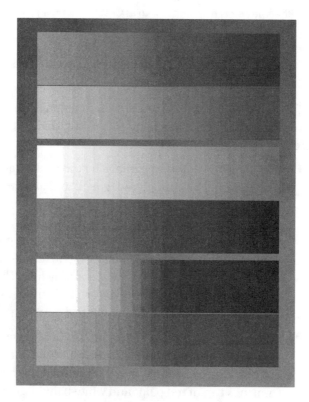

At the top are two strips showing a sliding scale of saturation, from unsaturated (at left) to fully saturated (at right). The upper strip's saturation has been altered by adding black; the lower strip's saturation has been altered by adding white.

In the middle are two strips showing the difference between brightening and darkening an image. The upper strip has most of its tones clustered at the light end of the scale, making it brighter. The lower strip has its tones concentrated at the dark end of the scale.

At the bottom are two strips that illustrate the idea of contrast. The upper strip has only a few different tones (about 16, actually) between the lightest and darkest areas, making it high in contrast. The lower strip has a continuous range of tones, giving it a lower contrast appearance.

These illustrations are simplified. You can examine the original images on the CD-ROM to better understand these basic concepts.

WARNING   What causes bad color? The chief culprits are: off-color light-sources (for example, taking pictures indoors by a fluorescent light, or outdoors at sunset), bad photofinishing (which produces prints that are too light/dark, off-color, or both), poor treatment of film (such as exposure to heat), mixed light sources (such as window light and interior room light), and faded colors (caused by failure of the dyes in color prints or slides after years of exposure to light or heat).

35 Slide Your Way to Good Color Balance

This technique works when your image has a slight color cast and doesn't need a major overhaul.

NOTE Photoshop can't add detail or color that isn't there. Color correction techniques work well with images in which all of the colors are present, but have too much of one hue or another. The extra color can be removed, leaving a well-balanced picture behind. Or, you can beef up the other colors, so they are in balance again. Photoshop does this by changing the value of some pixels that are close to the color you want and never truly adding any colors that aren't already there. So, if you have a photograph that is hopelessly and over-poweringly green, there may be no color left behind when you remove all the green. Or, you can add magenta until your subject's face turns blue (well, it won't happen that way), and all you'll end up with is a darker photo.

Here's the easiest way to fix color:

1. Choose Image ➢ Adjust ➢ Color Balance (or press Ctrl/Command+B) to summon the Color Balance dialog box.

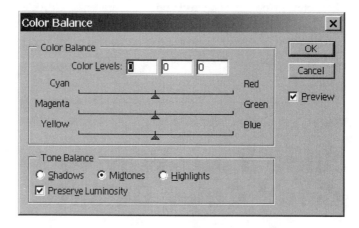

It has three sliders labeled Cyan/Red, Magenta/Green, and Yellow/Blue, for the three sets of complementary colors in the RGB and CMY (no K for black here) color models.

2. Choose Image ➢ Duplicate to create a second copy of the image for reference.

3. Choose whether you want to adjust the shadows, midtones, or highlights of an image by clicking in the appropriate radio button in the Tone Balance area of the dialog box. Images can have overall color casts (most easily fixed with the midtones setting), or they can be off-color only in the shadows or highlights.

4. Using either image, move the sliders to the left or right until you remove the color cast. You can compare the corrected image with the original version to make sure you're achieving the desired effect.

The sliders are so-named because when you add red, you are removing cyan; adding green removes magenta; adding blue removes yellow, and vice versa. It doesn't matter which way you work: if an image is too red, you can correct it by subtracting red.

If you want to be able to reproduce your color balance changes (say, you have several images taken under the same lighting at the same time), note the Color Level values at the top of the dialog box. The boxes record the amount of change for the red, green, and blue colors, from –100 to +100 percent.

36 Enrich Your Image's Saturation or Change Its Hue

You can also color correct an image using Photoshop's Hue/Saturation (and Lightness) control. The advantage of correcting color this way is that you can change the saturation of individual colors, or of all the colors in an image, without modifying the hue or lightness/darkness of those colors. The Color Balance method changes only the relationships between the colors.

Photoshop's Hue/Saturation controls let you change the richness of the colors in an image without modifying the individual colors, if you prefer. You do this by applying Saturation changes to the Master channel or main layer of an image. If you need to beef up just one color (say, to make your reds more saturated), you can do that too by changing the saturation of the red, green, blue, cyan, magenta, or yellow channels.

The Hue control modifies the overall balance of an image. If you visualize a color wheel like the one shown next, you can see how the Hue control changes the overall balance of the image (or one individual color layer, if you want) by rotating the entire palette one direction or another around the periphery of the color wheel.

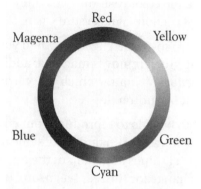

Move clockwise from red, for example, and the colors become gradually more magenta, then blue, then cyan.

The image shown in this figure isn't a bad picture, but it was taken on an overcast day and has an overall flat look.

If it were a black-and-white picture, we would only need to boost the contrast. However, that won't help the anemic colors. Photoshop's Hue/Saturation dialog box comes to the rescue here. Because our sample picture has such poor saturation, we'll adjust all the colors first.

1. Choose Image ≻ Adjust ≻ Hue/Saturation (or press Ctrl/Command+U) to view this dialog box.

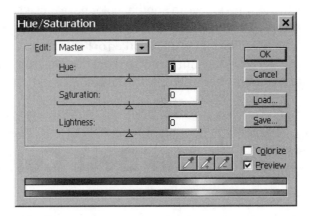

2. Change the Saturation value until the picture gains, in preview mode, the richness of color you are looking for. I used a setting of +40 for the example picture.

3. If the color is slightly off, experiment with the Hue control to find a setting that corrects any imbalance.

NOTE Moving the Hue slider (when the Colorize box is not checked) shifts the palette of colors around the color wheel. Slide it to the right, and colors move toward yellow, green, and eventually cyan at the 180-degree point opposite red on the color wheel. Slide the control to the left, and the palette shifts 180 degrees in the opposite direction, through magenta and blue before reaching cyan.

4. Monitor your adjustment by watching the two color bars at the bottom of the dialog box. The upper color bar shows the arrangement of colors prior to making modifications. The colors on the lower bar move, showing what color will be used to represent the hue directly above it on the upper bar after your change.

5. You can make adjustments to the brightness of the image by moving the Lightness slider. This varies only the relative darkness or lightness of all the colors in the image. If you want to change the contrast at the same time, you should use Photoshop's Brightness/Contrast control.

You may encounter images that can be improved by changing the hue, saturation, or brightness of one color only. You might have a holiday picture that needs to have its reds and greens enriched, but with muted blues. Perhaps the green grass and foliage in another color have picked up an undesirable color cast, and you want to shift all the green values one way or another to improve the color. Or, you may want to darken or lighten just one color in an image. Just select the color you want to modify from the Edit drop-down list, and apply the Hue/Saturation controls only to that color.

37 Choose the Best Color

Back when I worked for an advertising agency in Rochester, N.Y., I would pay big bucks for a color print from a professional color lab on the other side of town. At the time, the camera shop on the corner would have been happy to produce an 8 by 10-inch print for a few dollars. Why did I pay the extra bucks? My pro lab offered hand-made custom prints, produced one at a time with an enlarger and painstaking manual techniques. The exact color balance of a custom print is often crucial, so my pro lab routinely produced five or six variations, and let my clients choose the preferred examples. That's why custom prints are worth the extra money: you're paying not only for the handwork, but for the ability to choose from among several different prints. For critical advertising work, it's faster and more efficient for the lab to produce the variations all at once, and note the settings, than to go back and make tiny corrections over and over until the exact version you want is produced.

Of course, that was before Photoshop became a common tool at advertising agencies and other graphics shops. Photoshop's Variations option avoids hours of playing around with an image and never quite achieving exactly what you are looking for. After all, there's no guarantee that, after a lot of work, you might decide that an earlier version really did look better.

Photoshop's Variations are a sort of "color ring around" similar to what my pro lab produced. In this mode, the software itself generates several versions of an image, arranged in an array so you can view a small copy of each one and compare them. Photoshop's Variations mode is especially useful, so I'll use it to illustrate a third way to color correct problem photos.

Just follow these simple steps:

1. Choose Image ➤ Adjust ➤ Variations, to produce this dialog box.

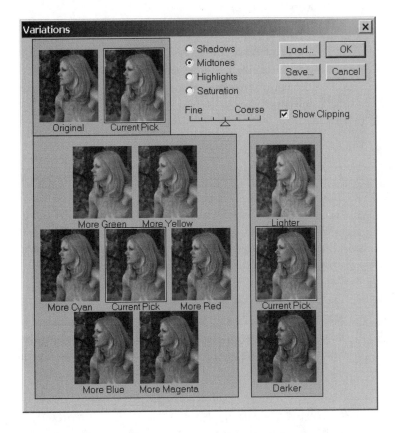

2. The Variations dialog box has several components:

◆ In the upper-left corner, you'll find a thumbnail of your original image (before modifications) paired with a preview of the changes you've made. As you apply corrections, the Current Pick thumbnail will change.

◆ Immediately underneath is another panel with the current pick surrounded by six different versions, each biased toward a different color: green, yellow, red, magenta, blue, and cyan. These thumbnails show what your current pick would look like with that type of correction added. You can click on any of them to apply that correction to the current pick.

◆ To the right of this thumbnail ring is a panel with three sample images: the current pick is in the center, a lighter version is above, and a darker version is below.

◆ In the upper-center of the dialog box is a group of controls that modify how the other controls are applied to shadows, midtones, highlights, and saturation. A slider underneath them specifies the coarseness of the variations. The coarser the setting, the more dramatic the changes are; the finer the setting, the more subtle they are.

◆ At the upper-right corner are buttons that let you apply or cancel your changes, and save or load settings.

3. If the Midtone button is not depressed, click it. You also want the pointer in the Fine...Coarse scale to be in the middle, and the Show Clipping button checked. When the latter is activated, any colors that cannot be modified further (that is, they are already as dark or as light as they can be) will be shown in the previews in a contrasting color.

N O T E You may Load or Save the adjustments you've made in a session so they can be applied to the image at any later time. You can use this option to create a file of settings that can be used with several similarly balanced images, thereby correcting all of them efficiently.

4. The example image is too cyan, so the More Red thumbnail will look better. Click it to apply that correction to the current pick. In fact, we needed to click twice, because the original image is very cyan.

5. The image is also too dark. Click the Lighter thumbnail.

6. Click the OK button in the upper-right of the dialog box when finished.

In this example, we worked only with the midtones. In most cases, the shadows, midtones, and highlights will need roughly the same amount of correction. In others, though, the shadows or highlights may have picked up a color cast of their own (say, reflected from an object off-camera). Photoshop's Variations options let you correct these separately if needed.

More often, though, you'll use the shadow-midtone-highlights option to improve the appearance of images that have too-dark shadows or washed-out highlights. Where any image editor's brightness/contrast control generally affects all the colors equally, this procedure lets you lighten shadows (bringing out more detail) or darken highlights (keeping them from becoming washed out) without affecting other portions of the image. The technique also lets you avoid nasty histograms and gamma curves.

38 Make a Test Strip

You'll find that Photoshop veterans most often use the techniques described so far in this section to make quick changes. The Color Balance, Hue/Saturation, and Variations controls don't offer the level of precision that serious graphics workers often need. But now that you've learned to use these capabilities, you're ready for a more professional tool, Teststrip, from Vivid Detail. A trial version is included on the CD-ROM accompanying this book.

Teststrip works something like Photoshop's own Variations tool, but it has many more controls and options.

Change All Colors

Teststrip's Ring Around mode is a lot like Photoshop's Variations, but it has many additional features. Follow these steps to explore them:

1. Choose Filter ➤ Vivid Details ➤ Teststrip to produce the tool's dialog box. The area in the upper-right corner has five buttons, each of which summon a different mode.

Click the Ring Around button to begin using the mode shown in this figure.

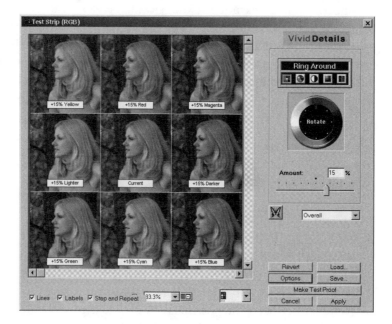

2. Adjust the Amount slider at the right center of the dialog box to control the amount of variation produced by the examples in the ring-around. This corresponds to the Fine/Coarse slider in Photoshop's Variations dialog box; but, of course, it has the advantage of showing you the exact amount of modification as a percentage.

NOTE The Amount slider can be set to positive and negative percentages. A positive value adds the specified hue; a negative value subtracts it. (Very cool!)

3. Choose Highlights, Midtones, Shadows, or Overall from the drop-down list immediately below the Amount slider to control the range of tones to which the changes will be applied.

4. Click in any of the variations to apply that modification to the current image. Do this as often as you like to optimize the image. If you change your mind, click the Revert button to return to the image as it was when you activated Teststrip.

5. If you already know your image needs a certain kind of correction—say, to add or subtract red, green, or blue or to make the image warmer or cooler—choose that option from the drop-down list at the lower center-right of the dialog box. Select Overall if you want to work with all colors (red, green, blue, cyan, magenta, and yellow).

6. If necessary, customize Teststrip's appearance. The check boxes and zoom controls at the lower edge of the dialog box let you:

◆ Show or hide white lines between the example images.

◆ Show or hide the labels displaying the Amount setting.

◆ Turn on or turn off Step and Repeat mode. When active, the examples are shown in a ring-around as the default. Turn off this mode to fill the preview window with the current image, as shown here.

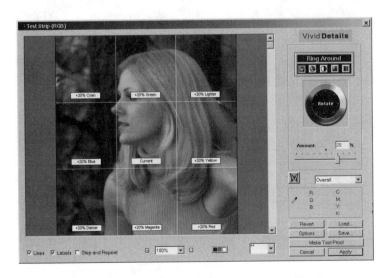

◆ To specify how much of the image is used in each example, click the plus and minus buttons, or choose a zoom setting from the drop-down list. Zoom in to work with a small area of your image, or zoom out to see the variations applied to all or most of the picture.

7. If you want to use a hue-style control like the one in Photoshop, Teststrip provides a color wheel in the upper-right corner. You can drag the pointer in this wheel to rotate the color palette as you do in Photoshop's Hue/Saturation dialog box. Note that the orientation of the color wheel is the reverse of the one shown in the "What's Wrong with This Picture?" section, which I created to correspond to Photoshop's Hue/ Saturation color bars. In practice, the difference means nothing.

Adjust One Color

Teststrip includes a One Color mode that lets you fine-tune colors of a single channel.

1. Click the One Color button in the toolbar at the upper-right. The dialog box changes to look like this one.

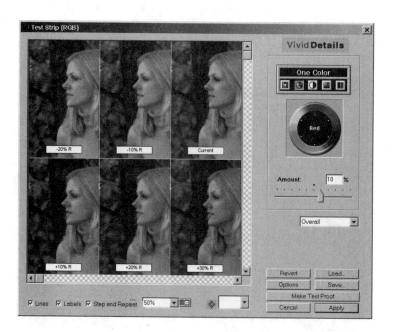

Many of the controls look the same, but some of them have different functions.

2. Choose the color you want to work with by rotating the pointer in the color wheel at the upper-right. Note that the wheel can't be rotated continuously: you must select red, green, blue, cyan, magenta, or yellow.

3. Select the amount of variation you want with the Amount slider.

NOTE Notice that the amounts shown by the labels in the preview window are now multiples of the value you choose with the Amount slider. That is, if you select 1 percent, the examples provide 1-, 2-, 3-, and 4-percent modifications (plus or minus). Choose 10 percent, and the examples show 10-, 20-, 30-, and 40-percent change (plus or minus).

4. The Lines and Labels check boxes and zoom controls work the same as in Ring Around mode. However, uncheck the Step and Repeat box when you want to fill the preview window with the image with the variations applied to that image.

5. You can choose the way the preview image is displayed by selecting an array from the drop-down list at the lower-right center of the dialog box. You can choose two to five vertical or horizontal "slices," each of an adjacent portion of the image (like a traditional photographic test strip), or divide the preview window into four, six, or nine boxes.

6. Apply your changes as before, by clicking the box in the preview window containing the modification you want to use.

Adjust Brightness/Contrast or Saturation

Teststrip includes two more modes for adjusting brightness and contrast, as well as saturation. Just follow these steps:

1. Click the Exposure button in the toolbar to produce the next dialog box.

2. Change the configuration of the preview using the same controls as in Step 5 above.

3. Click the Brightness or Contrast buttons, and then choose the Amount slider to apply a specific degree of brightness or contrast.

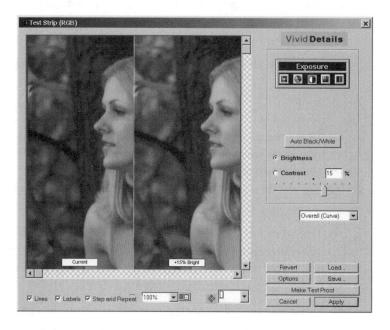

4. To adjust Saturation, click the Saturation button in the toolbar to produce this dialog box.

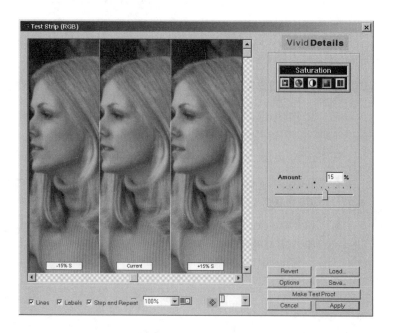

5. Use the Amount slider to make your modifications.

6. Click the Before & After button to view a preview showing all the changes you've made so far, accompanied by a list in the upper-right corner showing the values you've applied.

39 Create a Special Effect with Duotones and Tritones

Duotones and tritones are a time-honored way of increasing the number of shades of gray that can be reproduced with a printing press. However, true Photoshop fans aren't happy using time-honored techniques. We aren't really satisfied until we've subverted a perfectly good tool and used it for our own purposes. Here's how to create some duotones or tritones that you may not have seen before.

NOTE Using a single black ink and conventional halftoning techniques (wherein a photograph is converted to a pattern of dots), a printing press can reproduce only about 50 different shades of gray. When the dots become too large or too small, they become black splotches or white areas on the page. Duotone and tritone printing techniques apply ink to the same area several times, each using a different version of the image and a different set of dots. So, details too subtle to represent by a single halftone can be printed using a duotone or tritone image.

Follow these steps to see how it works.

1. If you're working with a color image, convert it to grayscale using Image ➢ Mode ➢ Grayscale. Photoshop's duotone effects can be applied only to grayscale images.

2. Select Image ➢ Mode ➢ Duotone to produce the Duotone dialog box.

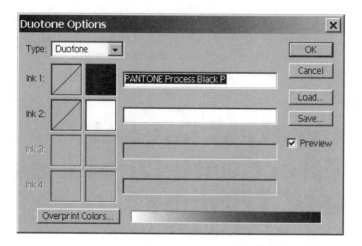

3. Choose Duotone from the drop-down Type list if it isn't already selected.

4. Click the boxes next to Ink 1 and Ink 2, and choose colors. You can use the conventional Photoshop Color Picker, or click Custom from the Color Picker dialog box and choose any Pantone colors.

If you actually intend to print your image as a duotone, you'll want to choose from among the Pantone spot colors, so your printer can match those colors using what is called the Pantone Matching System, a standardized way of specifying ink colors.

5. If you haven't selected a Pantone color, type in a name for your color.

So far the image doesn't look like much more than a toned grayscale image. But we can play with it to produce some interesting effects.

6. The box to the left of the color swatch for each ink is the Duotone Curve box. Click it to produce the following dialog box.

7. You don't need to understand how curves work to play with the tones using this dialog box (in fact, you'll probably feel freer to experiment if you don't). Move the cursor into the curve graph (the cursor will change to a crosshair), and drag portions of the curve up or down until you get an interesting effect. The bottom figure shows what the image looks like when only one of the colors is manipulated.

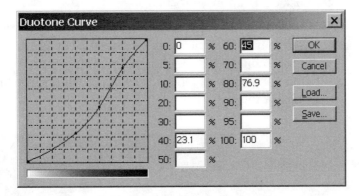

8. Click the Curves box next to the other ink color, and manipulate it as well.

9. Click OK to apply your changes.

10. Convert to RGB color, and make any additional modifications you want to fine-tune the image. For the final image shown in the next figure, I adjusted the brightness/contrast and then inverted the image for a unique two-color, almost solarized effect. The final image will look like this.

NOTE Tritones and quadtones work in much the same way, except (obviously) with more colors. Click the Load button in the Duotone dialog box to load some duotone presets that Photoshop includes.

40 Convert a Black-and-White Image to Color

Sometimes you have only a black-and-white picture when you need a color one, either to match other images in a project, or just for aesthetic reasons. You can create color images from grayscale pictures in Photoshop, and your results will range from OK to pretty good, depending on how much time you have to devote to the chore, and how artistic you are. However, even if you're no artist, you can achieve good results using the technique I'm going to show you. Just follow these steps:

1. Take a grayscale image and convert it to RGB color using Image ➤ Mode ➤ RGB Color.

2. Create a new transparent layer using Layer ➤ New Layer.

3. In the Layers palette, convert the blending mode of this layer to Overlay. That will allow the colors you apply to merge with the detail in the original image without obscuring it. This is a step that many would-be photocolorists don't know about.

4. Select a color to begin painting. In my example, I started by painting the hair of the model. Paint in the transparent layer using a soft brush.

   The most widely used way to choose hues for colorizing an image is a simple one: load a full-color image of a scene or subject that is similar in coloration to the colors you want. For a scenic, load a panorama picture. For a portrait, use a color portrait of the same person or another person. Then, with the example picture next to the image you're working on, you can use the Eyedropper tool to sample colors before painting each new shade.

5. After you've finished painting, adjust the opacity of the layer in the Layers palette to make the colors more subtle and lifelike.

6. Repeat Steps 2 through 5 to add all the colors you want for your image. You may have to adjust the opacity of each layer to blend the colors as you want them to appear.

NOTE Improve your color effect by using several layers, each with a variation on a particular color. For example, when painting faces, you will want to use four or five different flesh tones for the best realism.

7. Flatten the image. If you like, you can apply color correction techniques like those discussed earlier to improve the color rendition. I used this image.

Check out the black-and-white and color versions on the CD-ROM and the color insert to see the transformation. This image is a little primitive, but I wanted you to see what you could do in as little as five or ten minutes. Spend a half-hour colorizing a photo, and you'll really have something.

41 Make a Super Solarization

Remember the solarized pictures of John Lennon and the other Beatles from the end of the 1960s? If you were alive then and *don't* remember, perhaps you were partaking a bit too much of the era's *zeitgeist.* In any case, here's a quickie you can use to produce color-bending solarizations much more flexibly than Photoshop's own built-in filter. Just follow these steps:

1. Load a full color picture. I used the one I colorized in the previous project.

2. Choose Image ➢ Adjust ➢ Curves.

3. Drag the curve around to get a solarized effect you like. I made a U-shape, high at the left and right ends of the curve, and low in the middle to get the effect shown at the left in this figure.

4. Or, click the Pencil tool in the Curves dialog box and draw your own (very) wavy line to get a look something like the one at right in the figure.

Psychedelia comes and goes, but Photoshop creativity only grows and grows.

Transform Images

What you see isn't necessarily what you have to get in the digital realm. Photoshop lets you do a lot more than combine and retouch images or correct the color balance. You can transform images completely by changing the shape and size of portions of an image, adding a texture of brush strokes, or giving a harsh image a soft romantic glow. Many of these effects can be accomplished using Photoshop's built-in plug-ins or third-party tools like Eye Candy 4000, Xenofex, and Kai's Power Tools.

Using filters found in the Artistic, Brush Strokes, Pixelate, and Stylize submenus of the Filter menu, Photoshop makes it easy to generate effects that are strongly reminiscent of the styles of "real" artists. These kinds of filters have one thing in common: they reduce the amount of information in an image by combining or moving pixels. At first glance, the effect seems to be that of having turned a photograph into a painting. Instead of the harsh reality of the original image, we have a more organic, often softer picture that appears to have been created rather than captured.

However, in deference to true artists, including the art teacher at my children's school (who also happens to be their mother), I need to point out that just blindly applying filters helter-skelter won't produce true art. In a real painting, a brush stroke is applied in exactly the right size, shape, hue, and direction to provide a particular bit of detail from the artist's vision. Computers can't reproduce that insight. To get the best effects, a human—you—needs to remain in control of the creative process.

42 Mimic Cubism Without the Cubes

For this one, I looked high and low for images—literally—combining a sea-level photograph of the Atlantic North Coast of Spain with a shot of a trio of storks (actually, one stork cloned twice) captured in the highest provincial capital in Spain, Avila. Here's how I merged the two pictures and transformed them into a reasonable facsimile of a painting. If you want to follow along, you can find the original photos on the CD-ROM that is bundled with this book. I used Alien Skin's Xenofex filters, but Photoshop's native plug-ins can be used as well.

1. First, select the sky around the storks. The easy way to do this is to select the sky with the Magic wand (holding down the Shift key to select more and more parts of it), and then use Select ➤ Similar to grab the remainder of the sky.

NOTE Precision isn't critical because the stork background is a shade of blue similar to that of the sky in the seashore picture. Any stray bits will blend in well, especially after the pixel-pushing that follows.

2. Use Select ➤ Inverse (or press Shift+Ctrl/Command+I) to reverse the selection so it includes only the storks.

3. Press Ctrl/Command+C to copy the storks, move to the seashore image, and press Ctrl/Command+V to paste the storks down into the image.

4. Choose Edit ➤ Transform ➤ Resize, and make the storks any size you want within the composition. Drag them to a location you like, either heading out to sea or back toward shore after a long session of what-ever it is storks would do if they were sea-going birds.

5. Flatten the image to merge the storks and the seashore, and then make a copy of the layer using Layer ➤ Duplicate Layer.

6. On the upper layer, apply a filter to fracture the image into a lot of little pieces. I used Alien Skin's Xenofex filter, as shown in this figure.

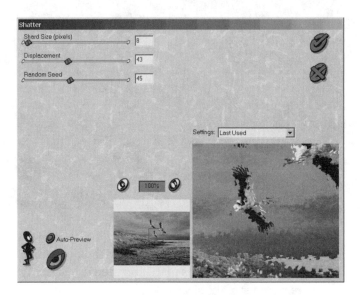

The most important parameter is the Shard Size slider. I used a small value to make the little pieces very small. The Displacement slider determines how far the pieces are moved from their original location. I used a value of 43. The Random Seed slider determines the random pattern; you only need to change this if you apply the filter to the same image multiple times and want different looks each time.

NOTE Photoshop's Stylize ➤ Tile filter can also be used to get a somewhat different effect. Experiment with the number of tiles to be used (80 to 99 are good starter values) and the kind of background between the tiles. I've used the Inverse Image setting with success.

7. Here's a step many forget to follow: Use Filter ➤ Sharpen ➤ Unsharp Mask, and accentuate the effect. Move the Amount slider until you get a pronounced brush-stroke effect. Usually 100 to 150 percent will do it.

8. OK, we've managed to fracture the stork/seagulls all to heck. You can restore them so they are recognizable. To do so, use a soft-brushed eraser to remove the shattered storks on the upper layer and reveal, at least in part, their unaltered cousins underneath. When you're done, the image should look something like this one.

43 Create Masterpieces with Master Strokes

Brush-stroke and painting-oriented plug-ins are by far the majority among Photoshop's native filters. However, you can't just blindly apply them, point to the results, and crow, "Hey, I meant to do that!" I can't count the number of times I've seen published examples of "computer manipulated images" in photography publications that were nothing more than straight photos with an ordinary Photoshop filter applied using the default settings. With a little creativity, you can go way beyond the ordinary. I'll show you all the things I was able to do with a single photograph.

This castle in Spain is perfect fodder for a digital painting.

Try these transmogrifications. Here are four variations on a theme:

1. The first thing to do is select the sky and save the selection. The sky and the castle in this photo need to be worked with separately because their tonal values are so different. Click the Add button in the toolbar (a sensational new Photoshop 6 feature) and then use the Magic Wand to select multiple areas, and Select ➢ Similar to make sure you grab every last pixel. If necessary, use Quick Mask mode (press **Q** to activate) and paint with a brush to grab any stray pixels. Then save the selection with Select ➢ Save Selection.

N O T E   Learn to use the New, Add, Subtract, and Intersect buttons in the toolbar. They're a dramatic improvement over earlier versions of Photoshop, in which it was all too easy to lose a selection when your finger slipped off a key or you clicked somewhere outside the selection.

2. To get the effect shown in the figure below, apply Filter ➤ Brush Strokes ➤ Angled Strokes. Use a very short stroke length, such as 3 to 5 to provide a lot of detail from the original image. Increase the sharpness to 6 or 8 so the strokes will be very clear. I used the Unsharp Mask filter to accentuate the effect even more.

NOTE When using Photoshop's various brush stroke filters, you should use small stroke or brush sizes to preserve as much detail as possible. For greater control, fade the filter after application by pressing Shift+Ctrl/Command+F. You can also apply the filter to a duplicate layer and adjust the opacity until you obtain the exact effect you want.

3. For the look in the following figure, use Filter ➤ Brush Strokes ➤ Ink Outlines. A brush stroke length of 1 looks good, but you'll want a lower Dark Intensity (around 9) and higher Light Intensity (I used 25) to keep the picture from being too dark and dismal.

Before applying the filter, I loaded the sky selection and copied the sky to a new layer, and then I processed the castle and sky separately so they both would end up with about the same degree of brightness, but with the castle having quite a bit more contrast. Sharpen both with Unsharp Mask to get the amount of detail you like.

4. The image shown in the next figure is one of my favorite Photoshop painting techniques. It uses the Brush Strokes ➤ Accented Edges filter.

Besides supplying a glow to the important edges of the image, setting the Edge Brightness slider to a high level (from 30 to 50) always generates some interesting pastel colors. The orange hue produced in this case really reproduces the sun-baked tone of Spanish structures of this sort. Use a small edge width to preserve detail.

5. The Dry Brush filter, found in the Artistic submenu, is an easy one to use effectively. You can play with the brush size, amount of detail rendered by the filter, and texture. I set the Brush Detail slider to the maximum (10) and the other two to the minimum (1) and added some sharpening to get the effect shown here.

44 Create Night from Day

This version looks great in black and white (it is a night scene, after all), but it really comes alive in full color, with a deep, rich blue night sky and eerie colors in the castle walls and along the horizon. I hope you'll check out the original on the CD-ROM bundled with this book. Here are the steps I took to produce this image:

1. Starting with the original image, I applied the Stylize ➢ Find Edges filter. There are no settings for this filter. Just apply it, and check out the results, which are shown in the following figure. As is, this effect is interesting enough to stand on its own. You could increase the contrast and brightness to create an image that looks like it was sketched.

2. Press Ctrl/Command+I to invert the image and reveal the night scene hidden within. If you like, you can load the sky selection you saved earlier and ramp up the contrast dramatically to produce the look shown next.

3. Press Ctrl/Command+U to produce the Hue/Saturation dialog box, and move the Saturation slider to between 80 and 100 percent to create a rich, eerie effect.

4. Load the sky selection, and make a copy of the sky area. Paste it down in a new layer.

5. Choose a very dark blue and a medium blue from the Swatches palette as the foreground and background colors.

6. Lock the transparency for the sky layer by clicking the Transparency box in the Layers palette (it's the left-most box just above the layers themselves).

7. Use the Gradient tool to apply a foreground-to-background linear gradient to the sky layer. Make sure the darkest blue is at the top, with the lightest blue at the bottom, near the horizon (simulating a "sky glow" effect).

8. Create a duplicate of this layer.

9. In the upper, duplicate layer, use Filter ➤ Noise ➤ Add Noise to add Gaussian monochromatic specks to the sky layer. Increase the noise value until the sky has the number of stars you'd like.

10. With the sky layer still active, choose Layer ➤ Add Layer Mask ➤ Reveal All to activate a layer mask.

NOTE When a layer mask is used, click in the Mask Layer thumbnail (at right in the layer) to work with the mask itself. Click the image thumbnail (at left) to work with the image.

11. Using the Gradient tool again, choose the Black-White gradient from the drop-down list in the Option bar, and apply the gradient to the layer mask, with the white at the top and black at the bottom. This creates a mask that reveals all of the starry sky at the top, but fades away to let the deep blue, starless sky of the layer beneath to show through at the bottom.

12. As a finishing touch, load the sky selection again, and press Shift+Ctrl/Command+I to invert it. On the bottom layer (which contains the castle image), make a copy of the castle. Click the top layer, and paste it down.

13. Apply the Outer Glow layer style, using the settings shown in the following figure. I set the size of the glow to 40 pixels, used a soft yellow as the background color, and added 42 percent noise to blend the glow in with the "noisy" sky. I set Opacity to 24 percent to further blend the glow and the sky. The result was a subtle amount of separation between the castle and the stars.

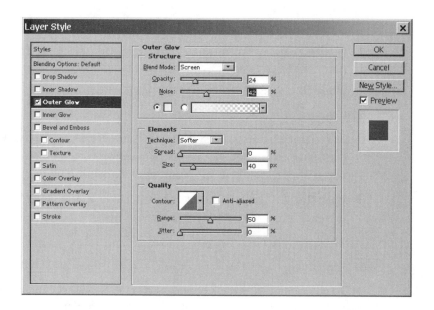

The resulting image, shown in this figure, looks pretty good in black and white, but it verges on the startling in full color. Check it out on the CD-ROM.

45 Create a Romantic Glow

Photographers have long known that a soft, diffuse glow adds a romantic look to portraits of women. Before digital magic became common, camera wielders resorted to placing bits of nylon stockings in front of their lenses, smearing petroleum jelly on filters, and using special lens attachments designed to hide or obscure facial flaws. Today, we can do the same thing, but with much greater control, using Photoshop. Consider this photograph.

The picture is nice enough as it is, even though there are slight hints of darkening under the eyes, a few stray wrinkles here and there, and a crease or two around the mouth. All of these defects may not survive the printing process—but trust me, they are there. Luckily, they can be banished in short order, using the following steps:

1. Use the Artistic ➢ Film Grain filter to add a kind of random noise to the image that resembles photographic film grain. The dialog box, shown in the next figure, has controls to let you adjust the amount of grain, the highlight area (in effect, increasing or decreasing contrast), and intensity (how strongly the grain overpowers the original image).

2. A better choice is usually the Distort ➢ Diffuse Glow filter (don't ask me why it's located in the Distort submenu). It produces a soft, glowing effect while adding a grainy texture. The dialog box has a Graininess slider, along with two more that can be a little confusing:

◆ The Glow Amount slider controls the size and intensity of the highlight glow. Adjust this too far, and you can completely wipe out your image.

◆ The Clear Amount slider controls the fuzziness of the entire image.

The finished images will look something like these.

The effect of Film Grain is seen on the left, and the effect of the Diffuse Glow is seen on the right.

3. Apply Diffuse Glow to other kinds of images, rather than strictly to portraits. The next figure shows a woodland scene that has been brightened and given a romantic look thanks to a judicious application of this filter.

46 Add Special Effects with Lighting

With lots of controls for you to play with and achieve many different creative effects, Photoshop's Lighting Effects filter, found in the Render submenu, is a mini-program in its own right. It can be used to apply both lighting (as if the image were being illuminated by a light source) and texture. Textures can range from subtle to outrageous and from matte to shiny and metallic. I decided to see what Lighting Effects could do to this mundane photo of a fledgling rock star in action.

Add Illumination

First, try out the illumination features of the filter:

1. Choose Filter ➢ Render ➢ Lighting Effects to produce the following dialog box.

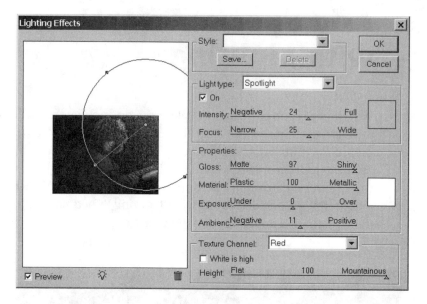

2. Select Spotlight from the drop-down Light Type list. Also available are Directional (less tightly focused than Spotlight) and Omni (which appears to be coming from all directions).

3. Adjust the intensity of the light and its other properties.

4. The ellipse in the Preview window shows the coverage area of the light and its point source (the handle in the center of the ellipse). You can drag the source to any point in the preview (even well outside the picture area, as if the light were located some distance from the subject) and drag the four side handles of the ellipse to change the shape of the coverage.

5. Click the Light Bulb icon at the bottom of the Preview, and drag into the preview area to create a second light source. You can specify light type, intensity, location, and other properties as with the first.

N O T E To turn on or turn off a light, select the light by clicking one of its handles, and then check or uncheck the On box.

6. Click OK to apply the lighting effect, and then boost contrast, if necessary, to end up with an image something like the one shown next.

Add Texture

Lighting Effects can also be used to add a texture to images. Follow these
steps to see some of the great things you can do:

1. Choose Render ➤ Lighting Effects from the Filter menu. Set up your
   lighting as before, using a spotlight and fairly dramatic lighting.

2. Set the Gloss slider to maximum Shiny. Set the Material slider to maximum Metallic. You can use the Exposure sliders to control brightness
   and the Ambience slider to adjust contrast, if you like.

3. Because this image is predominantly red, choose Red as the Texture
   Channel from the drop-down list at the bottom of the dialog box.

4. Click the White Is High box. This will make the lighter areas of the
   image "higher" in terms of the 3D texture you're applying, while the
   darker areas are "lower."

5. For maximum texture, move the Height slider all the way to the right
   to the Mountainous setting.

6. Click OK.

7. Adjust brightness/contrast, and sharpen to taste.

8. I added some flames using Eye Candy 4000's Fire filter to get the flaming fingers of fate shown in this figure.

Add a Spotlight

I used several different effects for the image shown in this figure. Lens flare adds an interesting effect, as if a spotlight were visible.

These are the steps:

1. Apply Lighting Effects, using a small amount of texture.

2. Add a lens flare with the Render ≻ Lens Flare filter, using the 105mm Prime, with brightness set to 100 percent. Drag the crosshair point on the preview window to position the light anywhere you like.

3. Select the background to the left of the guitarist, invert, and apply Eye Candy 4000's Corona filter behind him. I used a purple glow.

N O T E The Lens Flare settings are named after the effects you get with common wide-angle to telephoto lenses mounted on a 35mm camera when pointed toward a bright light source. A 50mm to 300mm zoom lens is a complex optic with lots of lens elements that let the light bounce around inside, producing a broad, fuzzy flare. A 35mm "prime" lens generates another sort of glare because it takes in so much light from such a wide angle. A 105mm "prime" lens creates a third type with its narrower angle of view and (generally) fewer optics inside the lens barrel.

47 Fix Faulty Perspective

Sometimes, twisting an image isn't done to create distortion, but to correct it. A good example of this is the need to fix pictures of tall buildings in which the structure seems to be falling backward. The problem in the following figure was caused by tilting the camera to take in the upper portion of the building. As a result, the bottom portion of the film plane is closer to the base of the edifice, while the top of the film is farther away. The only way to correct what photographers call *perspective distortion* in the camera is to use a special lens or a tilting camera back that will allow the film and subject to remain parallel even while the lens tilts.

However, Photoshop can do the same job easily if you know a few tricks. Here they are—applied to the image, a photo of a massive Roman arch at the top of a hill in Medinaceli, Spain. Because the arch is perched on a hill, the photographer couldn't simply back up and take the picture from a distance that didn't require tilting the camera. You may find yourself in a similar situation when doing architectural photography when your back is up against a wall (literally) and you can't move farther away or use a lens with a wider angle.

To correct the problem, follow these steps:

1. The first step is to increase the size of the canvas (this will give you a little room to stretch the archway in some new and interesting directions). Use Image ➤ Canvas Size, and increase the size by 125 percent in both horizontal and vertical directions. The exact amount doesn't matter because you're going to crop the image later anyway.

2. Choose View ➤ New Guides to create a horizontal Photoshop guideline. Drag it down near the base of the arch. Repeat, creating a horizontal guide that you drag down to just above the top of the arch.

Photoshop's selection tools let you extract the Eiffel Tower from Paris and transplant it to the Atlantic coast of Spain.

Four different photos were combined to create this fantasy landscape. You'll find out how to merge images like these in "Make Eye-Popping Graphics by Combining Images."

Color Gallery

Matching the lighting on the car to that of the surrounding area helps create a seamless composite. Create this image from the steps in "Make Eye-Popping Graphics by Combining Images," and then produce the enhanced version shown below on your own.

Don't like the hue of the car? Colorize it, and then blend it with the original automobile using Photoshop's Color Burn layer mode to preserve the fine detail.

"Retouch Your Images" shows you how to manually apply blur to selected areas of a sports snapshot to create the illusion of movement.

Flat images that are low in contrast can be improved by boosting the color saturation, as shown in "Correct Your Colors!"

Color Gallery

This is the "before" picture from "Retouch Your Images," prior to some major photo retouching to remove dust spots, facial blemishes, and an unfortunately tentative smile.

This is the same image with selective sharpening, blurring, some special attention to the eyes, and a glamorous softening effect added thanks to Photoshop's versatile Diffuse Glow filter.

Use Photoshop's Overlay layer mode to smoothly blend layers on which you've painted color detail with the original image. You'll end up with pastel colors that are still fairly lifelike, as described in "Correct Your Colors!"

Once colorized, a photo can be given a customized solarization treatment by manipulating its Curves, as described in "Correct Your Colors!"

"Retouch Your Images" will get you started with these effects.

Don't stop once you've created a special look, like the fifties postcard effect in the top image. A creative application of Photoshop's Posterize feature turned the landscape into a sixties psychedelic vista.

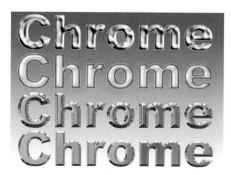

Eye Candy 4000's Chromium filter provides an endless variety of shiny metallic effects.

You can create a variety of colorful neon effects using Photoshop's Solarize filter and a bit of manipulation.

Looking for a logo for your pest extermination business? Eye Candy 4000's Chromium and Drip filters created most of the drama in this image. The "evil eye" at right was a normal human eye copied from a portrait and then given a high-contrast red treatment. Learn to create type effects like these in "Warp Your Words and Create Other Text Effects."

Look closely! Those birds are land-based storks headed out to sea in this image that creates a cubistic effect. You'll find out how to create these birds and the landscape below in "Transform Images."

The venerable Kai's Power Tools and its Planar Tiling and Glass Lens filters made it easy to convert a humdrum sunset photo into an otherworldly landscape.

Set the Edge Brightness to a very high level to get this unique look with Photoshop's Accented Edges filter.

The Find Edges filter creates a night look from a daytime image. Process the sky separately using the Add Noise filter to add a starry effect. Both of these effects are found in "Transform Images."

Color Gallery

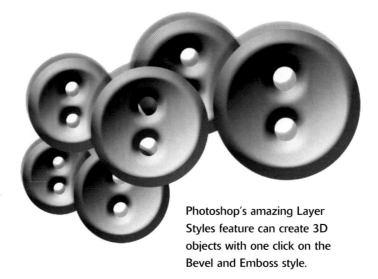

Photoshop's amazing Layer Styles feature can create 3D objects with one click on the Bevel and Emboss style.

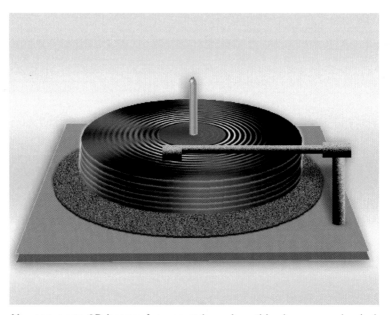

You can create 3D images from scratch, such as this obscure mechanical device used to play pre-CD music. The buttons and record player projects are both described in "Amazing 3D Effects."

Eye Candy 4000's Corona filter added the purple glow to this image of a budding rock star, as described in "Transform Images."

Photoshop's 3D Transform filter lets you wrap images around three-dimensional shapes, as shown in "Amazing 3D Effects."

Backlighting has an eerie, paranormal connotation, as fans of Moose and Squirrel (aka Mulder and Scully) and their popular television show know.

Eye Candy 4000's Fire filter was used to add this flaming effect to the text. These spooky type effects are described in "Warp Your Words and Create Other Text Effects."

It's important to match lighting, texture, shadows, and other elements when combining images, as was the case when a pumpkin and large rock were added to this elephant's habitat. You'll learn how to augment the pachyderm's environment in "Make Eye-Popping Graphics by Combining Images."

Ulead's Particle Effects filter has the amazing ability to let you position each and every one of the bubbles added to this image. You'll learn how to add bubbles to the castle in "Transform Images."

Don't have a digital camera? Just place a 3D object or two on the glass of your color scanner, and grab the image directly into Photoshop.

Moving the Eiffel Tower to the seashore is child's play compared to moving the seashore and Big Ben (actually, the tower that contains Big Ben, which is a bell) to a landlocked Spanish castle.

Can't move to get a better viewpoint? No problem. Photoshop lets you adjust the perspective of an image. This picture was taken down slope from an ancient Roman archway that surmounted a hilltop.

Photoshop's Distort capabilities straightened up the lines in this version. Add some clouds, and you have a picture postcard view. These two images are from "Transform Images."

The most mundane picture can be given a painterly appearance with built-in Photoshop filters and third-party filters. This is a "before" picture of the walls of a fortified medieval town.

By applying Eye Candy 4000's Swirl filter and boosting the contrast, you can make the image look like this. These images were created using third-party filters, as described in "Transform Images."

Type in a value other than the default 0-pixel position to place the guide's initial position away from the side of the canvas. That makes it easier to grab and drag.

3. Repeat Step 2, creating a pair of vertical guidelines. Your image will now look something this one.

4. Select the area to be corrected, and choose Edit ➤ Transform ➤ Distort. Using this mode instead of Transform ➤ Perspective gives you the flexibility to transform each of the four edges of the arch independently.

5. Drag the top handles of the selection until the top edge of the arch is parallel with the upper horizontal guide. Repeat with the lower handles and the lower horizontal guide.

6. Drag each of the sets of side handles to align the sides of the arch with the side guides. Your image should look something like the next one.

7. Crop the image into a rectangle. Use the Rubber Stamp tool (which we used a lot in "Retouch Your Images") to clone portions of the image to fill in any blank spots. You'll end up with something like the image shown in the top figure on the next page. But we don't have to stop there.

8. I selected the sky area with the Magic Wand (just as we did in the previous exercises) and applied Alien Skin's Xenofex Little Fluffy Clouds plug-in. The most important parameters for this filter are the Puff Size (in pixels) and Coverage (in percentage—the lower the percentage, the more your background sky will show through). The percentage, I used doesn't matter; select an amount that pleases you as you view the preview. This filter is far superior to Photoshop's own Clouds filter, which doesn't have controls and produces less realistic clouds.

9. Inverting my selection, I adjusted the brightness and contrast of the arch a bit, and added some sharpening. The finished image looks like the bottom figure on the next page.

Some clouds make the finishing touch.

48 Fill the Sky with Bubbles, Rain, or Snow

Here's a quickie that shows you how a fantasy image can be created quickly if you have the right plug-ins at your disposal. This one uses Ulead's Particle filter, a remarkably flexible plug-in that has lots of weather effects, such as Rain and Snow, as well as Firefly, Smoke, a decent Clouds filter, Fire particles, and a Star effect. I'm going to use several of these to get a couple different effects. The unmodified image of an ordinary, sunny day is shown here.

Let It Rain

To add rain to the picture, follow these steps:

1. First, select the sky area with the Magic Wand. It may take a few tries because the clouds make the process a little trickier. If necessary, use Quick Mask mode to paint or erase areas. Save the selection.

2. For a rainy effect, darken the sky and reduce the contrast using Photoshop's Brightness/Contrast controls. You can select a combination that varies anywhere between dismal (dark and low contrast) and forboding (dark, but with high contrast).

3. Apply the Ulead Particle Rain filter, using the dialog box shown in this figure.

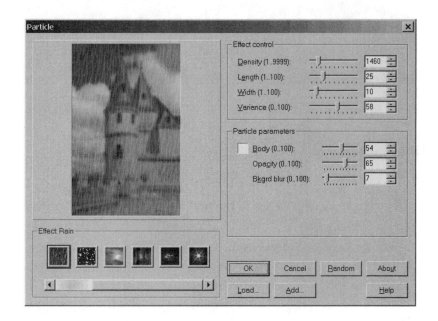

You can adjust the length and density of the rain, from a light drizzle to drenching sheets. Use the Opacity and Blur controls to adjust how much of the background image appears behind the rain.

4. Click OK to apply the rain effect. Your finished effect can be seen at the left in the following figure.

As you can see, rain and snow don't fall mainly on the plain in Segovia, Spain.

Let It Snow

You can always have a white Christmas with the following steps:

1. Work with a copy of the previously used image. Save the sky selection for reuse.

2. Select the sidewalk area in front of the castle, and apply a cloud filter to give it the look of being covered with freshly fallen snow. Fade the cloud filter so the paving underneath shows through.

3. Press **Q** to enter Quick Mask mode, and use a soft brush to select the tops of the towers, roofs, walls, and the bench. Press **Q** again to exit Quick Mask mode.

4. Use Ulead's Particle Effects Snow filter to dust snow on the selections. You may want to repeat the process two or three times to add enough snow. Just remember to click the Random button each time you visit the dialog box so the snow will be dusted in a different place each time.

5. Press Ctrl+A to select the entire image, and apply the snow filter to the overall scene once or twice. Your finished image will look like the one on the right in the previous figure.

Add Tiny Bubbles—Or Huge Ones

Here are the polka steps that would make Lawrence Welk happy:

1. If you'd rather have bubbles instead of rain or snow, activate the sky selection you saved.

2. Apply Ulead Particle Effects' Bubble filter. Adjust the Density (number of bubbles overall), Size (the maximum size a bubble can be), Variance (the percentage difference between the largest and smallest bubbles), and other parameters.

3. You can apply the filter several times. Press Random between applications to place the bubbles in a new location.

NOTE The filter displays the bubbles in a preview window, as seen in the following figure. Amazingly, you can select each bubble individually and move it around the window. Do this when you find that a bubble obscures some portion of the image you don't want covered. You could, for example, apply the bubbles to the entire image and move the ones that blocked important parts of the castle.

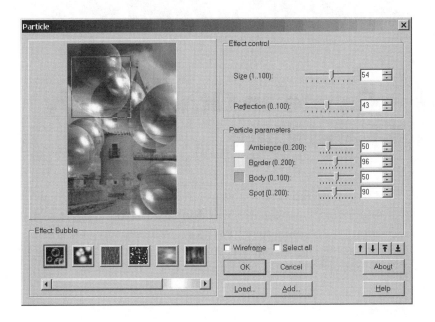

4. Apply the filter several times if you want. The next figure shows the final image with the bubbles applied only to the sky (on the left) and overlapping the castle with custom-arranged bubbles (on the right).

49 Create an Otherworldly Landscape

I'm going to show you how to put a whole raft of tools to work to create an otherworldly landscape. You don't even need to begin with a sensational picture. I'm going to work with an ordinary sunset scenic picture, like the one shown next. You can use your own, if you like. You'll need Kai's Power Tools, version 3.0 or later, to perform this magic trick.

The Planar Tiling filter used here is also furnished with some later versions of KPT, but the program may not install it for you automatically.

1. Start with the basic image, and create a duplicate layer.

2. Apply the Planar Tiling filter, choosing Perspective Tiling from the dialog box. KPT will create multiple copies of the image and squeeze them all down into the lower half of the picture, arranged in a perspective layout with a horizon halfway up from the bottom of the image, as shown here.

3. Arrange the original, unmodified layer so it extends above the horizon, as you can see in the next figure. The image is already starting to look otherworldly.

4. Create a circular selection on the unmodified background layer, and copy it to a new layer of its own.

5. Apply the KPT Glass Lens filter, using the Bright mode. Adjust the Opacity so the original image still shows underneath.

6. Use Photoshop's Burn toning tool with a large soft brush, and darken the lower left side of the sphere, adding some shading.

7. I duplicated the sphere layer, filled it with black, applied a vigorous Gaussian blur, and then used Edit ➢ Transform ➢ Scale to flatten the layer into a shadow. I made the shadow's opacity around 20 percent and moved it to the left and beneath the sphere to enhance the hovering effect.

8. Finally, I applied an Outer Glow layer style, using a soft yellow hue to provide separation between the sphere and its background. The image, which radiates a science fiction tone, looked like the one shown next.

9. If you want a really eerie effect, add the Eye Candy 4000 Electrify filter to the sphere, using short electrical tendrils to give the object a "plasma sphere" look. You can see that variation in this figure, which has a spacey, "plasma" look.

Amazing 3D Effects

Many of the best features of Photoshop 6 are designed to help you move your flat, uninteresting images into the third dimension. Without some 3D effects, many images just lay there like ancient Egyptian tomb drawings. Fortunately, you can easily make your images jump off the page or screen by using Photoshop's built-in effects, techniques you can learn, third-party 3D tools such as Corel Bryce, or even your scanner.

50 Create 3D Effects with Your Scanner

You can create great-looking 3D effects with your scanner by grabbing scans of 3D objects and then manipulating them in Photoshop to make them appear to jump off your image. Here are a couple of projects that will show you how 3D scanning works and will give you some ideas of what to do with them.

Things you scan don't have to be flat! I grab images of three-dimensional objects all the time for eBay auctions, and you can use your scanner to get 3D images for any Photoshop project. The advantages of scanning 3D objects are that you don't have to use a conventional camera or a digital camera and a scanner is quite a bit faster for grabbing an image than either alternative. I can scan an image into Photoshop in 30 seconds or less. It takes a lot longer than that to set up lighting and then transfer an image from my digital camera to Photoshop.

N O T E The maximum thickness of a 3D object that can be scanned successfully varies by the scanner. Most scanners have sufficient *depth-of-focus* (the distance that an object can be from the scanner glass and still appear sharp) to successfully scan half an inch or more. More inexpensive scanners using a newer type of sensor may have very limited depth-of-focus. These sensors are called *contact-image sensors* (CIS) because the sensor moves at a much smaller distance to the glass than conventional scanners, and the original must be, more or less, in contact with the glass to be captured sharply.

Here are some tips for scanning 3D objects:

◆ Make sure your scanner glass is clean.

◆ Lay the object on the glass carefully to avoid scratching the glass.

◆ If you want a white or light-colored background, drape a piece of paper over the object. That will provide smooth shadows that conform to the shape of your object, as shown in this figure.

Don't rely on the white cover of your scanner; it is probably dirty and will create uneven shadows because some parts of the object will be much farther from the background than others.

◆ For a dark background, just leave your scanner cover all the way up, as you can see in the next figure.

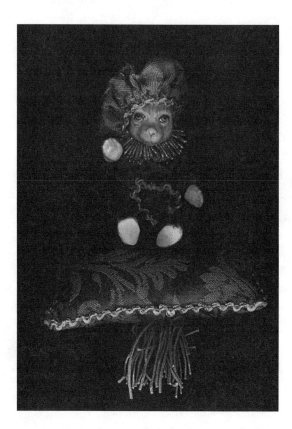

◆ Parts of the object that are farther away from the glass will receive less illumination and will appear darker. This effect is referred to as *light-falloff*. This is most apparent with objects that are relatively "deep" or "thick" compared to their width, as you can see in the left-hand bunny candy dispenser in the next figure.

Use Photoshop's Quick Mask feature to paint a soft mask onto the darker portions. Then use Image ➢ Adjust ➢ Levels, or you can use Image ➢ Adjust ➢ Brightness/Contrast to even the tone, as you can see in the right-hand bunny in the next figure. (Check out the original on the CD-ROM bundled with this book to see how dramatic the difference can be.)

51 Create Rough, Realistic 3D Holes

Here's a clever way to put a scan of an object with some holes onto your page.

1. Grab some pieces of corrugated cardboard, and tear a few artistic-looking holes in them. I used cardboard with a white upper surface and a brown underside, for contrast. Brown-on-brown cardboard doesn't create a look that is quite as dramatic.

2. Scan the pieces. Place some black paper behind the hole to make it easier to select the aperture later in Photoshop. I used 300dpi resolution, which is plenty to work with, but it doesn't produce an extra-large file size.

3. In Photoshop, use a soft, white paintbrush to paint around the edges of the hole to fade it out to pure white. Set the Opacity of the brush to 25 percent to simplify producing a fade-out effect. One result of this technique is to make it easy to place this graphic on a Web page with a white background; it will seamlessly blend in.

4. Use the Magic Wand or your favorite selection technique to select the hole itself. The Magic Wand plus Select ➤ Similar will usually grab all the pixels in the hole, while leaving the rest of the image alone (this is the reason you used black paper instead of white).

5. Create a new layer, and fill the hole selection with white.

6. Use Layer ➤ Layer Style ➤ Inner Shadow to create a shadow "under" the hole that makes it look as if it were cut out. (You can also use Eye Candy's Cut Out filter, if you like.) In the dialog box shown below, work with these controls:

◆ Manipulate the Opacity slider to make the inner shadow more or less dramatic. I used a value of 89 percent.

◆ Use the Distance slider to adjust how far the shadow casts into the hole from the edge. I used 10 pixels for my setting.

◆ The Size slider controls how blurry the shadow is, and, therefore, how large it is. I used a 16-pixel setting to produce a soft, but still distinct shadow.

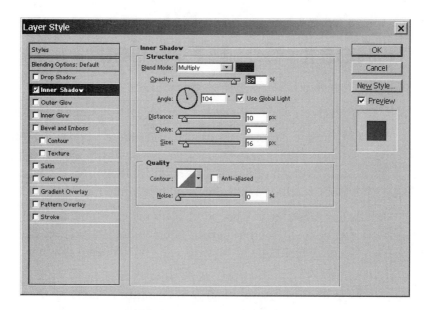

7. If you like, you can add a little random noise to the shadowed hole to give it a little texture. I used Filter ➤ Noise ➤ Add Noise, and then I specified 4 percent monochrome Gaussian noise in the dialog box.

8. Flatten the image and use it the way it is, or add some text to create a logo, Web page button, or other distinctive artwork, as shown in the following two figures.

NOTE   You'll find more about creating 3D text looks in "Warp Your Words and Create Other Text Effects" and tips for using Photoshop to enhance Web pages in "Working on the Web."

52   Make Realistic Buttons and Screw Heads

Photoshop and its plug-ins have plenty of button and bevel tools you can use to create decent-looking raised 3D objects from scratch. Add a few drop shadows (and Photoshop 6's Drop Shadow layer style makes that easy), and you have a good-looking object. Use these techniques to achieve a look that goes beyond the cookie-cutter button look everyone else is using.

Screw Heads

To make realistic screw heads, just follow these directions:

1. In an empty layer, hold down the Shift key while you drag with the Elliptical Marquee tool to create a perfect circle.

2. Use the Gradient tool to fill the circle with the radial gradient of your choice. I used the Copper gradient style to provide a metallic effect.

3. For a more realistic 3D effect, use Photoshop's Spherize filter, KPT 3's Glass Lens, or Eye Candy 4000's Glass plug-in. I used KPT 3's Glass Lens in this case because I like the kind of highlight it provides.

4. Add texture using Photoshop's Texturizer tool (Canvas or Sandstone, with very low Relief values, on the order of 2 or 3) or, as I did, simply add random noise using the Filter ➤ Noise ➤ Add Noise plug-in.

5. For a hard-edged screw, leave the screw head the way it is. To produce a rounded-edge screw, apply Photoshop's Bevel and Emboss layer style. Set the Soften slider to 5 pixels to make a rounded edge rather than a true bevel.

Your basic screw heads, *sans* grooves, will look like this.

You can use either one to get in the groove, so to speak, using these steps:

1. Make a thin rectangular selection across the center of the screw head, copy it, and paste it down into a new layer. Paste it down twice more.

2. Use Photoshop's Brightness/Contrast control separately on each of the three layers.

◆ Use the Brightness slider to make the top layer of the three layers about 25 percent darker.

◆ Use the Brightness slider to make the next layer down 85 percent darker.

◆ Use the Brightness layer to make the bottom layer of the three layers 75 percent brighter.

3. Select the middle and bottom layers separately, and use the cursor arrow keys to nudge them up 5 or 6 pixels and down 5 or 6 pixels, respectively. This creates a carved 3D effect, as if the layers were a groove. The farther up or down you move the "light" and "dark" layers, the deeper the groove will appear to be. Your screw head will look like the one at left in this figure.

4. You can flatten the image to finish the slot-head screw, or you can continue with the next steps to produce a Philips-type screw head.

A Philips screw head is not much harder to create. Just follow these steps:

1. Merge the three groove layers down to a single layer by making all three visible, selecting the top layer of the three layers, and then pressing Ctrl/Command+E twice to merge them.

2. In the groove layer, click with the Magic Wand outside the groove, and then press Shift+Ctrl/Command+I to invert the selection to the groove itself.

3. Choose Select ➢ Modify ➢ Smooth and a pixel value that will round off the edges of the rectangular groove. This amount will vary depending on how large your groove is, but a value of about half the width of the groove is a good start. For my 10-pixel high groove, I used a value of 10.

4. Use Shift+Ctrl/Command+I to invert the selection again, and then press the Delete key. That will remove everything outside the selection, giving you a rounded-end groove.

5. Duplicate the groove layer and then rotate it 90 degrees counterclockwise. Place the vertical groove on top of the horizontal groove.

6. Select the area where the two overlap, and press Delete to remove it. Your Philips-head screw will look like the right-hand image in the previous figure.

Create a Real Button

Working on a sewing-oriented Web site? How about some buttons that look like…buttons? Even if you're not building a Web site you might want to achieve a realistic button look. Although you could do it with earlier versions of Photoshop, the new layer styles make this a no-brainer, if you know what to do.

1. In an empty transparent layer, create a circular selection by holding down the Shift key as you drag with the Elliptical Marquee tool.

2. Fill the circle with a dark-to-light linear gradient, using either black and white, or your choice of colors as the foreground and background shades.

3. Apply the Bevel and Emboss layer style, as shown here.

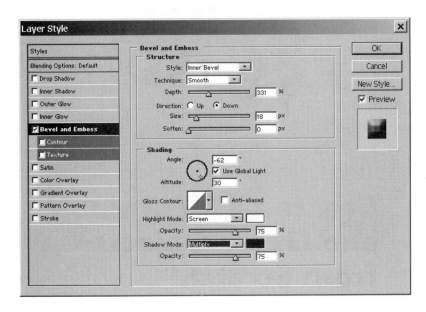

◆ Choose Inner Bevel to produce an edge for the button.

◆ Select Smooth for Technique to create a rounded edge.

◆ Click the Down button to make the disk concave.

◆ Move the Depth slider to adjust the amount of concavity. I used 331 percent to assure a pronounced concave effect.

◆ Adjust the Size slider to control the width of the edge of the button. I used 18 pixels.

4. Use the Elliptical Marquee tool to select a buttonhole, and press Delete. Repeat for the second buttonhole. (Do this four times if you want a four-hole button—just be sure to make each hole smaller.)

Notice that the layer style applies to each of the holes you create, so they have the same concave shape as the button itself. This really cool effect is the result of Photoshop's Layer Styles capability!

You'll end up with buttons like the ones in the array shown in the following figure.

53 Create a 3D Turntable and Other Objects from Scratch!

Although most of the projects in this book are small but eye-opening explorations into Photoshop's often unexplored capabilities, in the real world you'll most often have to put together a lot of different techniques. The next exercise puts a whole raft of tools to work to create the phonograph record turntable shown in this figure.

Although the final image may look remarkably lifelike, it was created entirely from scratch in Photoshop. I'll show you how to reproduce this object, of course, but you'll probably find the tricks more useful in building realistic objects of other types. Because the entire project is more complex than most in this book, I'll break it down into easy-to-handle pieces.

Create a Record

The first step is to create a phonograph record (aka "LP") and then learn how to give it a 3D appearance through the use of perspective.

1. In an empty transparent layer, create a perfect circle by holding down the Shift key as you drag with the Elliptical Marquee tool.

2. Fill the selection with a radial gradient, using the Copper preset from the drop-down list in the Option bar.

3. Choose Filter ➤ Distort ➤ ZigZag, and select Pond Ripples from the drop-down list in the ZigZag dialog box.

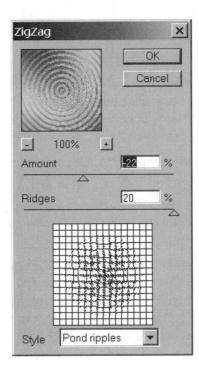

4. Set the Amount slider to –22 percent to produce a concentric groove effect, and set the Ridges slider to 20 percent in order to generate a whole bunch of them.

NOTE In real life, a record doesn't have multiple concentric grooves: it has one groove that spirals from the outer edge to the center. However, it's easier to get an even-looking appearance doing it this way. You can't get the right kind of spiral with Photoshop's built-in tools.

5. Using the Rectangular Marquee tool, select the upper half of the disc, using the center point as a guide. Copy the top half and paste it down.

6. Use Edit ➤ Transform ➤ Flip Vertical to flip the top half, and then move it down to cover the bottom half of the disk.

7. With the upper layer active, press Ctrl/Command+E to merge the two halves of the disc.

8. Choose Image ➤ Adjust ➤ Invert to reverse the tones of the disc. Use the Brightness/Contrast control to your taste to make the disc look more shiny and record-like.

9. Create a new transparent layer above the disc. Using the Elliptical Marquee tool, click in the exact center of the disc. Hold down the Alt/Option and Shift keys while dragging to create a circle around the center of the disc. Make it large enough to resemble a record label.

10. Fill the selection with a color (I used Red). If you want a more realistic label, add some text.

11. In the Layers palette, change the opacity of the label's layer to about 85 percent. You should be able to see through the label to the disc underneath.

12. Use the Brush tool with a small, hard-edged brush (the size will vary depending on how large you've made the record; the brush should be big enough to resemble the hole in the center of a long-playing record). Using white as your foreground color, click in the exact center to make a hole in the record.

13. Merge the visible layers by pressing Shift+Ctrl/Command+E. Your completed record should look something like this one.

Make a Stack O' Tracks

The next step is to create a pile of LP records, as if they were stacked on a turntable. This is where we learn how to create a 3D effect using Photoshop's perspective tools.

1. Select the disc, and then choose Edit ➤ Transform ➤ Perspective.

2. Drag the handles at the corners to warp the disc into a perspective view, with the handles closer to each other at the top than at the bottom. The disc looks like the one shown next.

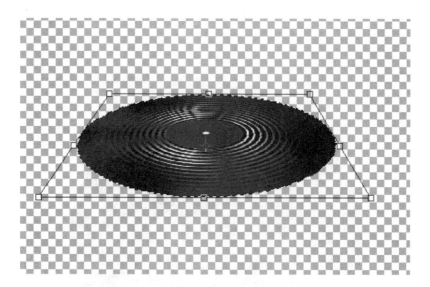

Press Enter to apply the transformation.

3. With the disc still selected, choose Layer ➤ Layer Style ➤ Outer Glow. Use the values shown in this figure to create a faint glow around the edges that will help separate each disk from the ones below it.

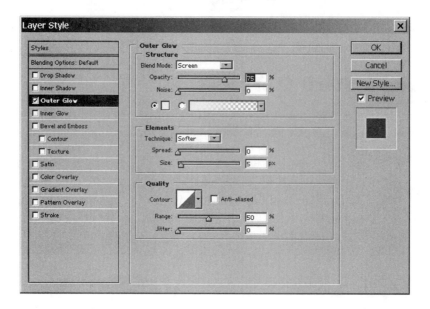

4. Duplicate the layer six or seven times to create a set of records. Nudge each layer a few pixels above the layer below it to arrange them into a stack, like the one shown here.

Construct a Turntable Platter

Records don't spin by themselves. They need a turntable platter.

1. Create one more duplicate layer of the discs, and then use Edit ≻ Transform ≻ Scale to enlarge it slightly to produce a turntable under the whole stack.

2. Use Edit ≻ Fill, and fill the larger turntable disc with 50 percent gray from the drop-down list in the Fill dialog box. Lock the transparency for the layer before you do this, or check the Preserve Transparency box in the Fill dialog box.

3. Add some random noise (you should know the drill by now) to give the turntable a texture.

4. Duplicate the turntable layer, and fill the original (lower) layer with black, using Edit ≻ Fill with the Preserve Transparency box marked.

5. Nudge the darker layer down a few pixels to give the turntable some thickness. Your turntable will now look much like the one shown next. Delete the glow effect from the turntable layers.

Combine Layers into a Manageable Set

You're in the home stretch now. You've learned enough to coast through creating the other components of a record player turntable. This is the perfect opportunity to learn about Photoshop 6's new Layer Sets capability, too.

1. With the Rectangular Marquee tool, create a rectangle large enough to serve as the base for the turntable. Fill it with 50 percent gray using Edit ➢ Fill.

2. Duplicate the layer, and use the Brightness/Contrast control to darken it.

3. Nudge the lower layer a few pixels down to finish the turntable base.

4. If you like, you could merge all the visible layers by making the top layer active and pressing Shift+Ctrl/Command+E. However, Photoshop's new Layer Sets capability provides an easier way to reduce the number of layers you have to manage at one time, while preserving their "editability." Choose New Layer Set from the Layers palette's flyout menu, and type in a name, such as **Stack of Tracks**.

5. A folder named "Stack of Tracks" appears in the Layers palette. Click each layer you want to add to the set in turn, and drag it into the folder. You'll see the layer text indented slightly, indicating that it is part of the layer above, as shown in the left side of this figure.

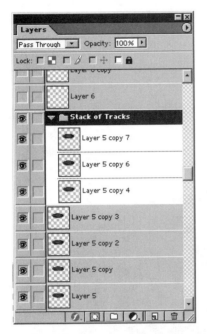 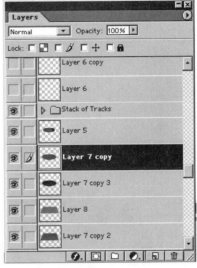

Note that the layer order needs to be the same inside the folder. You may have to reorder the layers after dragging into the set.

6. Click the down-pointing triangle (▼) in the layer set's layer to collapse the layers into a "closed" folder, effectively hiding them from view, as shown at right in the previous figure. Even so, you can open the layer set at any time, and edit the layers.

Add the Finishing Touches

Just follow these easy steps:

1. On a new transparent layer, create a thin vertical selection with the Rectangular Marquee. Make the selection about the size of a spindle that would fit through the holes of the record stack.

2. Choose Select ➢ Modify ➢ Smooth, and specify a value of about five pixels to round off the ends of the spindle.

3. Fill the spindle with a linear gradient, or do as I did and use Eye Candy 4000's Chrome plug-in.

4. Nip off the end of the spindle, and move it above the record stack, positioned as if it were going into the hole in the records.

5. Repeat Steps 1 through 3 to create a tone arm in four tubular segments, as shown here.

Then merge the layers to create a single layer holding the tone arm.

6. For the ultimate in realism, create shadows for the spindle and tone arm. Duplicate the spindle and tone arm layers. Fill the lower versions with black, and apply a Gaussian blur. Rotate the spindle's shadow counterclockwise by 90 degrees, and use Edit ➢ Transform ➢ Skew to stretch the tone arm's shadow to a realistic angle.

7. Flatten the image, and you're done.

54 Wrap an Image Around a 3D Object

Wouldn't it be great if you could "wrap" an image you created around a 3D object in Photoshop? You could, for example, create a globe by taking a map and wrapping it around a sphere, as shown in this example.

Or, you could mock up a new package for a product by creating the package front and then wrapping it around a 3D rectangular shape. It really would be great, but Photoshop doesn't quite have the tools—yet! The biggest drawback is that Photoshop's 3D Transform plug-in lacks lighting controls. So, once you've wrapped an image around a shape, it doesn't look all that much different from before—just twisted out of shape a bit.

Because of its limited capabilities and confusing controls, some Photoshop guides have only a paragraph or two covering 3D Transform—usually lumped in with the other Rendering filters. But don't panic! I'll show you how to do some actually useful things with this capability, relying on Photoshop's other capabilities to make up for some of the missing features.

The globe in the previous figure was fairly easy to create. I took a flat, 3D map of Australia, and placed it on a sphere using the 3D Transform dialog box.

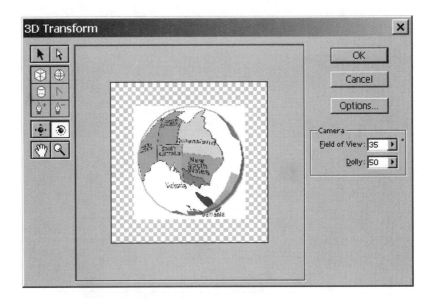

I'll show you how to use its options in the project that follows. After I created the basic globe, I used Photoshop's Lighting Effects plug-in to provide the lighting the 3D Transform tool lacks. Then I applied a halo around the globe (the Outer Glow layer style) and some clouds.

While globes are a ball, let's try something a little more challenging: creating a package mock-up for an advertising campaign.

1. The first step is to create the packaging itself in 2D form, as shown in the next example.

I won't spell out each and every step, as you use most of these techniques elsewhere in this book. (Take a special look at "Warp Your Words," the next chapter, for tips on the text effects used here.)

◆ Fill an empty layer with a radial gradient using the Orange-Yellow-Orange Photoshop preset (available from the drop-down list in the Option bar).

◆ Create the **ALL NEW** text, warped into an arc with the Text Warp feature, which is discussed in the next chapter. Then apply a drop-shadow layer style.

◆ Create the **PRIDE** text with the Rise Text Warp feature, fill it with random noise, and then stroke the edges with dark green paint 10-pixels wide.

◆ Add **NOW INCLUDES H$_2$O** text, with a drop-shadow added, and a background star created with Eye Candy 4000's Star plug-in.

The fonts, colors, settings, and actual text aren't important. You can vary the effects all you like to create your own packaging, or use the Pride file from the CD-ROM.

2. Crop the packaging artwork into a tall box shape, and paste into a new empty layer. Make sure there is enough room in the layer to move the artwork around as you rotate it. If necessary, use Image ➤ Canvas Size to increase the area you can work within.

WARNING When working with the 3D Transform filter, it's always best to create a new layer. The filter can render on the current layer, but the transmogrified image will tend to blend into the background. Place it on its own layer where you can work with it further.

3. Choose Filter ➤ Render ➤ 3D Transform to produce this dialog box.

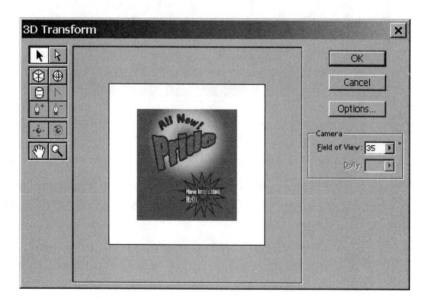

Your artwork will appear in the preview window of the 3D Transform dialog box.

4. Click on the Cube icon at the left side of the dialog box. You can also choose from sphere and cylinder shapes.

5. Drag in the preview area to create a cube-shaped framework, known as a *wireframe.*

6. To make the wireframe conform to the shape of the artwork, you'll need to drag three of the handles to three corners of the artwork's rectangular shape. I've put arrows in the following figure to show you which handles go where. Use the white arrow (at the top right of the dialog box's tool palette) to move the handles.

7. The fourth handle controls the "thickness" of the cube. Move it so it makes the shape relatively thin, as shown next.

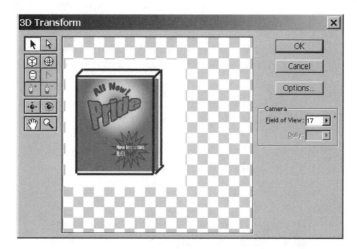

(I've exaggerated the wireframe lines in the illustration so it will show up on the printed page; in real life, the wireframe is a set of thin green lines.)

8. Click the Options button in the dialog box, and unmark the Display Background box. That will allow you to view your artwork wrapped around the shape, without any of the background that might remain showing.

9. Four controls at the bottom left of the dialog box let you pan the viewpoint of the shape (as with a camera) from side to side and up and down, rotate it in 3D space as you would with a trackball, move the shape around, and zoom in and out. Use the trackball control to rotate the shape, as shown in the next figure.

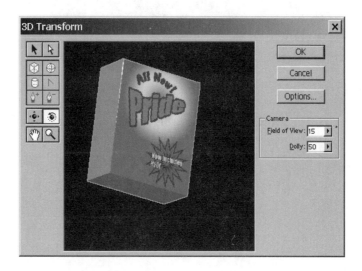

10. Click the Options button again, and choose rendering and anti-aliasing quality from the drop-down lists. If you're just experimenting, leave them both set at Low for the fastest rendering speed. When you're ready to lock in your effect, set them both at High for maximum quality.

11. I finished my mock-up by adding a drop-shadow layer style and a multicolored background to get the final image. Your final image will look like this.

55 Import 3D Graphics from Other Programs

If you want the most flexibility in working with 3D objects in Photoshop, consider importing your three-dimensional graphics from another program, such as Corel Bryce, Caligari trueSpace, and SoftImage 3D. However, these programs can be prohibitively expensive (some of them, such as Alias Wavefront's Maya, are priced in four-digit territory) because they include animation tools that you probably don't need.

However, you can still buy some 3D applications for under $50, including Ulead's Cool3D, a trial version of which is included on the CD-ROM bundled with this book. The key to making the most of any 3D program you have access to is to do all the lighting, shading, texturizing in the original application. Make sure you choose the viewing angle in the original application, too. Then, save a copy in the application's native format, and export an image in a form Photoshop can read. That way, you'll be able to return to the 3D file and make modifications if there are some changes you need to make that can't be done in Photoshop.

Cool3D is a perfect tool for learning how to work with Photoshop in conjunction with 3D applications. It's relatively easy to learn (even though it does boast a mind-numbing set of features), and it creates high-resolution BMP files (in addition to compressed GIF and JPEG format files) that Photoshop can read with no trouble.

Although doing justice to Cool3D would take an entire chapter, at minimum, and a full book of this size for more complete coverage, this project will get you started. The goal here is to demonstrate how you can quickly create 3D text and objects and export them to Photoshop. Install Cool3D from the CD-ROM, and we're ready to get to work.

1. Launch Cool3D. You'll be faced with this daunting workspace.

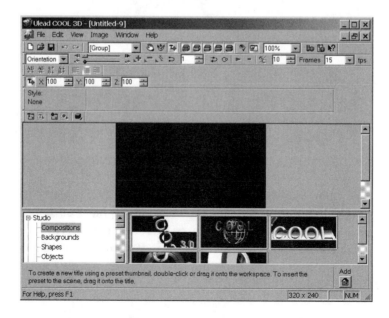

2. Cool 3D offers several ways to put objects in your working window. Insert text, graphics, or a geometric shape by clicking the buttons immediately above and to the left of the working window. From left to right, they are:

Insert Text A window pops up for you to enter and format text.

Edit Text Active only when text has already been entered.

Insert Graphics Produces a pop-up mini-drawing program with tools you can use to create shapes of your own fiendish design, including polygons, ellipses, and complex shapes.

Edit Graphics Active only when there are graphics to be edited using the drawing module.

Insert Geometric Shape You can choose Sphere, Cube, Cone, Cylinder, or Pyramid from a drop-down list.

3. Alternatively, you can choose objects from Cool3D's libraries, available from a scrolling collapsing/expanding list in the lower-left corner of the workspace. The options appear in a preview window to the right of the libraries; just double-click a selection or drag it into the working window.

4. You can insert multiple objects and work with them individually, giving each its own texture, orientation, color, or other attributes.

5. Freely change the position, rotation, and size of each object using the tools on the Standard (top) toolbar.

6. Finally, apply any of the special effects, bevels, textures, backgrounds, and other options available from the scrolling Libraries window. The next figure shows a typical example of what you can do.

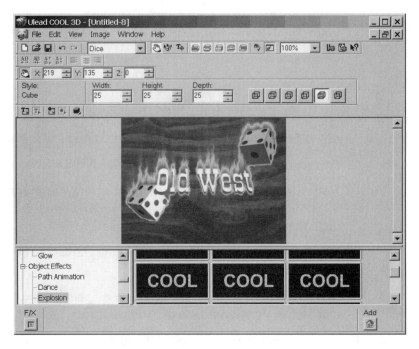

7. Save the file in BMP format by choosing File ≻ Create Image Files ≻ BMP File. You can load this file into Photoshop and work with it further.

8. Save a version in Cool3D format, too, for later work.

NOTE Don't apply a background within Cool3D if you think you might want to create your own in Photoshop. You'll avoid tediously separating your text or objects from its Cool3D background manually.

If you decide you want different effects or need to reorient your objects, just reload the Cool3D version and make your modifications. This figure shows some alternative versions of the original artwork.

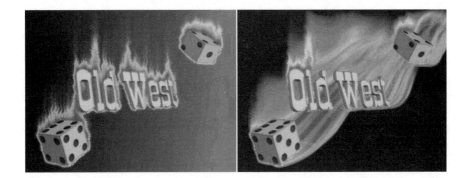

Warp Your Words and Create Other Text Effects

Pictures catch the eye, but well-chosen and well-presented words capture and hold your attention. A spectacular photo will alert you to an interesting story in the newspaper, but the headline is what convinces you to read it. Graphics on a Web page may help establish a theme or aid in navigating the site, but the text conveys the real information. Photoshop 6 has some new tools that let you create stunning logos, distinctive Web text, captivating captions, and engaging headlines. Used carefully and with taste, warped words can add something special to every graphic.

56 Great Metallic Text Effects

Metal is more than just heavy: it conveys a high-tech appearance, adds substance, and just looks cool. This section will show you how to create a variety of interesting metal looks for your text.

Make a Shiny Aluminum Nameplate

A shiny metallic surface can serve as a basis for many other effects, including brushed metal, pitted or corroded metal, and similar looks. Start out with this shiny aluminum nameplate, and then let your imagination loose.

1. Choose the Text tool (or press **T**), and click the Create A Text Layer button on the toolbar.

2. For best results, choose a font with thick strokes that will show off the metallic texture. Arial Black creates a bold, clean look.

3. In a transparent layer, type your text.

N O T E Large text often looks better when the spacing between the letters is less than that used for paragraph text. In the Character palette, click the tracking drop-down list and choose a negative value (such as –25 or –50) to move all the characters closer together.

4. Make sure your text is correct, and fix any typos now.

5. Click the Commit button in the Options toolbar (you can also "set" your text by choosing any other tool in the Tool palette), and then change your characters from editable text to pixels by choosing Layer ➤ Rasterize ➤ Type.

6. Choose the Linear Gradient tool, and select the Black, White gradient from the Gradient Picker on the toolbar.

7. In the Layer palette, select the Lock Transparency box. This will ensure that the gradient is applied only to the text and not to the background.

8. Click on the left side of the text, and drag to the right side to apply the gradient.

9. Duplicate the layer by choosing Layer ➤ Duplicate from the Menu bar. This new layer will appear *above* the original layer.

10. With the Linear Gradient tool still active, click on the right side of the original (lower) layer, and drag to the left.

11. Use the Move tool (press **V** to switch to it from the keyboard), and nudge the lower layer two or three pixels to the left and two or three pixels upward.

12. Select the upper layer, and choose Image ➤ Adjust ➤ Brightness/Contrast from the Main Menu bar, and change the values to produce exactly the kind of metallic sheen you want.

13. If you like, use Filter ➤ Render ➤ Lens Flare to add a sparkly highlight or two.

Your nameplate should look something like the following figure. I added my own gradient background to make the effect show up better.

Create Copper Text

If you'd rather have a brushed copper look, you can add a few steps to the previous procedure and get the look shown here.

1. Choose the Text tool, and click the Create A Text Layer button on the toolbar.

2. As before, choose a font with thick strokes that will show off the copper texture.

3. In a transparent layer, create your text.

4. Click the Commit button on the toolbar.

5. Change the text to pixels by choosing Layer ➢ Rasterize ➢ Type.

6. Choose the Linear Gradient tool, and select the Copper gradient from the Gradient Picker.

7. In the Layer palette, select the Lock Transparency box. This will ensure that the gradient is applied only to the text.

8. Click the top edge of the text, and drag down to the bottom edge to apply the gradient.

N O T E Hold down the Shift key so the gradient will be applied at a perfect right angle.

9. Duplicate the layer by choosing Layer ➢ Duplicate from the Menu bar. This layer will appear above the original layer.

10. Choose the Black, White gradient from the Gradient Picker.

11. On the original (lower) layer, click the right side of the text and drag to the left.

12. Use the Move tool (press **V** to switch to it from the keyboard), and nudge the lower layer two or three pixels to the left and two or three pixels upward.

13. Select the upper layer again, and choose Filter ➢ Texture ➢ Texturizer, and select Sandstone from the drop-down list. Adjust the Scaling slider to 50 percent and the Relief slider to a value of 2. Then click OK to apply the texture.

Your nameplate should look something like brushed copper.

57 Generate a Chrome Effect with Eye Candy 4000

You can generate metallic effects even more quickly if you have Alien Skin's Eye Candy 4000, a version of which is available on the CD accompanying this book. This plug-in's Chrome effect can be used to produce much more than just a simple chromium sheen, as you can see in the following figure.

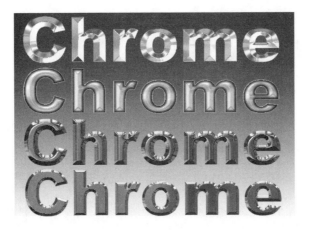

You can fashion dozens of cool chrome looks using the three tabs on the Eye Candy 4000 Chrome dialog box. Here are some instructions for creating each of the effects shown:

1. For a chiseled effect like the one shown at the top in the Chrome example, choose Carve from the Bevel Profile tab, the Silver Reflection Map, and then adjust the Bevel Width, Bevel Height Scale, and Smoothness to get the exact look you want.

2. For a more fluid look (like the second example from the top in the Chrome example), select Subtle Button from the Bevel Profile tab, choose the Silver Reflection Map from the Basic tab, set Bevel Width to the maximum, and set both Bevel Height Scale and Smoothness to a value of around 30.

3. For a glasslike effect, such as the effect in the second from the bottom example in the Chrome example, choose Button from the Bevel Profile tab, the Outdoor Reflection Map, and set both the Bevel Width and Bevel Height Scale sliders all the way to the left. Move the Smoothness, Ripple Thickness, and Ripple Width sliders all the way to the right.

4. If you'd rather have a flat nameplate, like the bottom text in the Chrome example, use the same basic settings, but move the Smoothness slider all the way to the left.

In the Chrome dialog box's Basic tab, you control the kind of reflection applied to the chrome, the kind of bevel (if any) around the selection, the smoothness, the nature of the ripples in the surface (if you want ripples), and other similar effects.

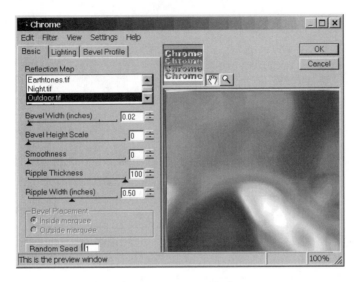

In the Lighting tab, you adjust the direction, brightness, and color of the light used to create the 3D chrome effect.

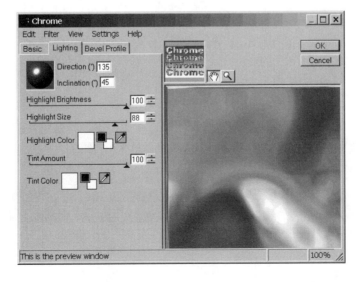

The Bevel Profile tab makes it simple to fine-tune the geometry of the bevel around your text or selection.

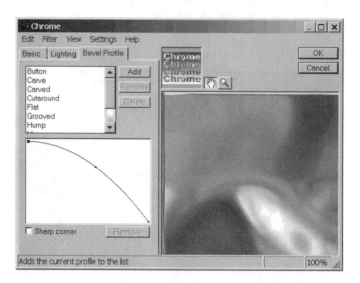

58 Eerie Backlit Text

Nothing is quite as eerie as backlit text on a black background. Often, the text and background are both black (or another dark color), so the text is visible only because of the ghostly backlighting around its edges. However, you can also get a scary effect with white text, as you can see in my parody logo, shown here.

(Remember that parodies like the ones in this section are OK when used for humorous or illustrative purposes, but you generally can't appropriate someone's trademarked logo for your own use.) For this exercise, I'm going to show you how to create a different logo that smacks of the paranormal.

1. In a new image, press **D** to change the default foreground/background colors of Photoshop to black and white (if they are not set to those values already).

2. Fill the background with black (Edit ➤ Fill, using Foreground Color is a quick way to do this). Make this layer invisible by first double-clicking the layer name to turn the background into an ordinary layer and then clicking the Eyeball icon next to it.

3. Choose the Text tool, enter the text you want to backlight using a relatively large point size (72 to 144 points), and click the Commit button. I created a large letter *Z* for this example.

4. Choose Layer ➤ Rasterize ➤ Type to convert the editable text to pixels.

5. Select Layer ➤ Duplicate Layer to create a copy of the text you just made.

6. Select the original layer of text (it will be located underneath the duplicate layer in the Layers palette), and choose Layer ➤ Layer Style ➤ Outer Glow to produce the dialog box shown here.

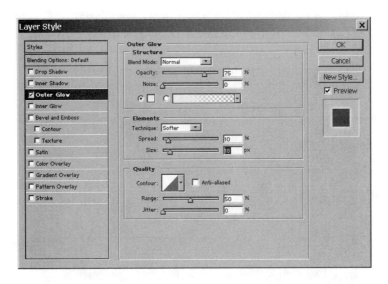

You'll be using this layer as the backlighting for the text.

7. Adjust the nature of the backlighting with this dialog box. The most important parameter is the Size slider in the Elements area of the dialog box, which sets the size, in pixels, of the backlight glow. The larger the number, the more diffuse the effect. I used an 18-pixel setting to produce a healthy, but not too diffused, glow.

8. Click in the Color box in the Structure area of the dialog box to choose a color for your glow from Photoshop's standard Color Picker. The button next to the Color box must also be checked.

NOTE You can experiment with the other settings to see what they do (although with a backlighting effect like this one, the changes will not be readily apparent). You can, for example, change the opacity of the glow, but that won't do much to our black-on-black text. Adding Noise adds a weird speckle to the glow.

9. Click OK to apply the glow.

10. To simulate the logo of my favorite TV show, I used Filter ≻ Distort ≻ Ripple on the black text and added a white text overlay.

11. Make the all the layers visible to see what the effect looks like, as shown in the final image displayed in this example.

59 **Warp Text**

Photoshop 6 now includes a powerful Text Warp feature you can use to bend type to your will. The interesting thing about this capability is that you can warp text in various ways *before* you have *rasterized* it (converted it to pixels instead of editable text). That means you can correct typos or adjust the text in other ways as you warp it, rewarp it, or dewarp it. Photoshop gives you 15 different ways to warp your words. The following exercise shows you how to distort your text in three interesting ways:

1. In a new image, choose the Text tool, and type the words **Over the rainbow** or the text of your choice.

2. Click the Create Warped Text button to produce the next dialog box.

3. For a rainbow effect, choose Arc from the drop-down list.

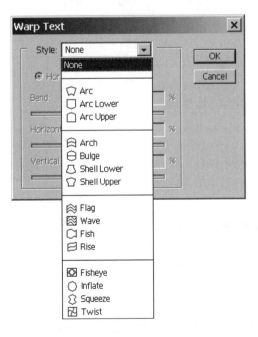

4. Type **Under the weather**, click the Create Warped Text button, and choose Arc Lower.

5. Type **WAVE THE FLAG**, click the Create Warped Text button, and choose Flag from the drop-down list.

6. Convert each of these text layers to pixels, and apply other effects of your choice—as I did for this figure.

Don't forget to lock the transparency of each type layer before applying styles and fills.

Over the Rainbow   I filled the text with a rainbow gradient, then I used the Bevel and Emboss layer style.

Wave the Flag!   I applied a custom red/white/blue gradient (you learned how to create gradients in "Transform Images"), and gave the image a 3D look by applying the Bevel and Emboss layer style with the Pillow Emboss style.

Under the Weather   The only thing needed to achieve this look was Xenofex's Crumple plug-in. I used Crinkle Size and Distortion, both set to values of 30. A trial version of Xenofex 1 is included on the CD with this book.

7. To finish off the examples, I merged the visible layers (Layer ➤ Merge Visible) after I turned off the background visibility. Then I applied a Drop Shadow layer style, and I added a background of a blue-white gradient (top to bottom) with some clouds added with Photoshop's Filter ➤ Render ➤ Clouds filter.

Photoshop's other Warp tools include:

- ◆ Lower and upper arcs (in which the most pronounced bend is applied to the bottom and top of the text, respectively)
- ◆ Arch (for a less-pronounced effect than arc)
- ◆ Bulge
- ◆ Shell upper/lower (which can give you a pie-wedge effect)
- ◆ Plus some choices with effects that are self-evident, including Wave, Fish, Rise, Fisheye, Inflate, Squeeze, and Twist

All have slider controls to let you modify the amount of the effect. The following figure shows an example of each.

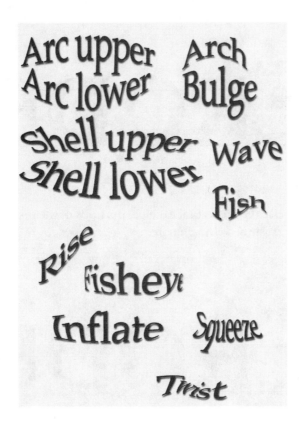

60 Erode Some Text

Creating eroded and weathered text is easy! Just follow these steps:

1. Create your text on a transparent layer, and rasterize it using Layer ≻ Rasterize ≻ Type.

2. Give the text the 3D look of your choice. I used the Bevel and Emboss layer style with some softening dialed in with the Soften slider (the amount of softening, which Photoshop measures in pixels rather than as a percentage, will vary depending on what size type you use) to create the weathered look shown next.

![ERODE text with weathered 3D bevel and emboss effect]

3. Use the Lasso tool to select portions of the text to simulate cracks and erosion, as shown here.

Hold down the Shift key to select multiple areas.

4. Save the Selection using Select ➢ Save Selection.

5. Copy the selected area of text, and paste it down in a new layer. If necessary, nudge it so that it is in exactly the same position as the original image area.

6. Use the Bevel and Emboss layer style again. Set the Depth slider for a high amount (making the erosion as deep as you like), and move the Soften slider to 0 pixels. Click OK to apply the layer style to get the effect shown at the top of the following figure.

7. For a really weathered look, use Filter ➢ Stylize ➢ Diffuse, as I did in the enlarged example at the bottom of the next figure.

61 Ignite Flames and More

Although many third-party add-on filter sets have flame, fire, and ice plug-ins, you'll find that you can achieve effects that are as good—or better—using Photoshop's built-in tools. Plus, these "scratch-built" effects are more customizable because you know exactly what went into making them.

Basic Flames

I'm really going to pile on the flaming effects in this one. You don't have to use them all to achieve looks that range from burning embers to a raging inferno. Just follow these steps:

1. On a transparent layer, enter the text you're going to set on fire, click the Commit button, and rasterize the text into pixels.

2. Choose the Gradient tool, and select the Orange, Yellow, Orange gradient.

3. Lock the transparency for this layer in the Layers palette, then fill the text with the gradient.

4. Use Image ➤ Rotate Canvas ➤ 90° CW (Clockwise) to turn the image on its side.

5. Unlock the transparency for this layer in the Layers palette.

6. Apply the Filters ➤ Stylize ➤ Wind filter. Use the Blast and From The Right settings.

7. Turn the image back to its original orientation with Image ➤ Rotate Canvas ➤ 90° Counterclockwise.

8. You may or may not want to erase some of the flame artifacts produced by the Wind filter. You might find the extra flames interesting, or you might find them distracting.

9. Copy the layer, and apply the Inner Glow layer style to the lower layer.

10. With a black background added, the text will look something like this.

 (Trust me, it looks a lot more impressive in full color! View the image on the CD-ROM packaged with this book.)

Singed Text

Perhaps you only want to singe your text a little. Here's a quick way to do that:

1. Create your text, and fill with the Orange, Yellow, Orange gradient as you did in the previous Steps 1 through 3.

2. Make a duplicate of the image.

3. Choose Image ➤ Mode ➤ Indexed Color from the menu bar. Click OK when the Merge Visible Layers And Discard Hidden Layers dialog box pops up. Then click OK to accept the default values for the Indexed Color dialog box.

4. Choose Image ➤ Mode ➤ Color table to produce the Color Table dialog box.

5. Select Black Body from the Table drop-down list. The Black Body color table is a set of colors produced by an object when it is heated, and it works well with any fire or flame effects you want to create.

6. Select the entire image, and paste it into the duplicate you made in Step 2.

7. Choose the original layer (not the one you just pasted), and select the transparency of that layer—the background. You can use the Magic Wand, but a more reliable way is to choose Select ➤ Load Selection, and then click the Transparency entry in the Channel drop-down menu. Click the Invert box within the Load Selection dialog box so that only the background is selected.

8. Switch to the layer you pasted, and press Delete to remove the background, leaving the "singed" text on a transparent layer.

9. You can save the selection to be safe (you're going to reuse it shortly); however, if you don't choose any other tools, the selection will be preserved through the next couple of steps.

10. Using the Swatches palette, choose a bright red and orange as your foreground and background colors (click the first patch, then Alt/ Option-click the second patch).

11. Create a new layer under your singed text, and choose Filter ➤ Render ➤ Clouds to generate a flaming smoke look. Because your selection is still active, the background is applied only to the area not occupied by the text (hide the text layer temporarily if you want to check).

12. Okay, here's the really cool part, so pay close attention. Choose Filter ➤ Distort ➤ Ocean Ripple from the menu bar, and apply it to the "clouds" background you just created. Flatten the image, and you'll end up with impressively combusting text, like the text shown in this figure.

(Again, you'll have to check the original on the CD-ROM to be suitably amazed.)

Flames: The Easy Way

If you have Eye Candy 4000 (included on the CD with this book), Eye Candy 3, Ulead Type Effects, or any of the many other third-party packages that offer a flame effect, achieving realistic flames is almost too easy. I created the effect shown here to show you how simple it is.

1. Create your text on a transparent layer, as before, and rasterize it.

2. Apply the Orange, Yellow, Orange gradient to the transparency-locked layer.

3. Unlock the transparency for the text layer, and choose Eye Candy's Fire plug-in.

4. You can experiment with the values shown in the dialog box pictured here.

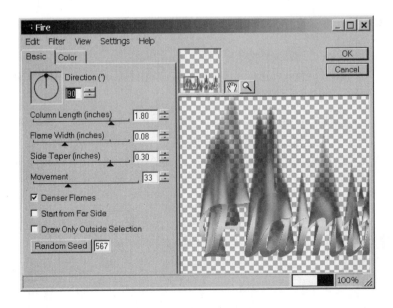

Click OK to apply the modification. Your finished text will look something like this.

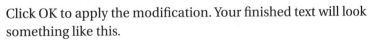

Flaming effects like this are almost too easy with Eye Candy.

62 Fast Frozen Text

You can create frozen text as easily as flaming text—if you know the right tricks. Here's how to do it:

1. Create your text on a transparent layer, as you did earlier in this chapter.

2. Lock the transparency for the text, rasterize it, and apply the Copper gradient we used earlier.

3. Choose Image ➢ Adjust ➢ Desaturate to turn the copper tone to a grayscale color.

4. Unlock the layer, and use Filter ➢ Texture ➢ Texturizer to apply a sandstone texture to the text. Set Scaling to 100 percent and Relief to a value of 10 to create a nice 3D effect.

5. Choose Image ➢ Adjust ➢ Hue/Saturation, and click the Colorize box.

6. Set the Hue slider for 250 (a deep blue), set the Saturation slider at 15, and then click OK to color the text.

7. Duplicate the text layer.

8. Choose Image ≻ Rotate Canvas ≻ 90° CW (Clockwise).

9. Press **Q** to enter Quick Mask mode, and select the upper text layer.

10. Use a soft brush to "paint" a mask on the top surface of each letter in the text (or the right side of the rotated text). Paint about 25 percent of the height of the letter, as shown next.

11. Press **Q** again to exit Quick Mask mode.

12. Choose Filter ≻ Stylize ≻ Wind, and select Blast and From The Right. Click OK to apply the filter.

13. Choose Image ≻ Rotate Canvas ≻ 90° Counterclockwise to return it to its original orientation.

14. Select the bottom text layer (the one which has not had the Wind filter applied to it) and choose Image ≻ Adjust ≻ Hue/Saturation again, and move the Lightness slider to the right until the frosty upper surface of the text takes on the appearance you like. Click OK to apply the change.

15. I used the Bevel and Emboss layer style set to Emboss to produce the final effect shown next.

63 Dazzling Neon Effects

Where would urban night-time advertising be without neon signs? What smoky lounge or college dorm room could exist without them? Why should your Photoshop artwork lack the subtle glow of neon? You can create dozens of neon-like effects with Photoshop—all built around the same basic techniques described next.

1. Create a new layer (press Shift+Ctrl/Command+N), and fill it with black.

2. Using white as your foreground color and a sharp-edged brush, draw some artwork on the black layer, or create some white text, then rasterize it, and merge it down with the black layer (you should have the text rasterization routine down pat by now).

NOTE A text font with round edges, such as the Plump MT font I used, works really well with neon effects. It simulates the smooth curves of the neon tubes. Use a bold font in a large size. This effect does not work well on thin fonts in smaller sizes. Similarly, when drawing your neon shapes, try to avoid sharp corners.

3. Apply a Gaussian blur to the white-on-black text or drawing. Use a heavy blur setting, such as the 7.5 pixels I used. If you happen to be working with a high resolution image or with very large text/strokes, you may need to use more blurring. In this example, I also applied the Bulge setting of the Text Warp tool (before I rasterized it) to create a rounded look.

Try for approximately this much blurring—more, and your text will become unreadable when "neonized."

4. Apply the Filter ➤ Stylize ➤ Solarize filter to reverse some of the tones, leaving an outline of your text or drawing. If your text becomes almost or entirely filled with black, you probably have forgotten to merge the text with the black layer below it. You can also get an undesirable look if you choose a font that is too small or that has strokes that are too thin.

NOTE *Solarization* is an old photographic technique in which partially developed film is exposed briefly to light, reversing the tones of some of the image. The process gives you a weird half-negative/half-positive image. Photoshop achieves the same look without the chance of accidentally ruining your film. In the darkroom, solarization was pretty much a trial-and-error process.

5. Choose Image ➤ Adjust ➤ Auto Contrast (Alt/Option+Shift+Ctrl/ Command+L) to produce the true neon glow.

6. Add neon-like colors by using Image ➤ Adjust ➤ Hue/Saturation. Click the Colorize box so you can add your own colors. First, move the Saturation slider all the way to the right, so your neon colors will be especially vivid.

7. Then slide the Hue control until you get the neon hue you like. Green, red, and purple work especially well. Move the Lightness slider a little to the left for a slightly different look, with the white neon "bulb" more subdued.

Bumping the contrast up produces a true neon look.

8. Play around to achieve different looks. At the top of this image, I applied the Glowing Edges filter to the solarized text, and then I added a radial gradient. At the bottom, I used Glowing Edges, added Ulead's Particle Effects Star filter, colorized the lettering, and finished off with Image ➤ Adjust ➤ Auto Levels.

Streamline and Supercharge Photoshop

Photoshop's actions capability, considerably beefed up for version 6, lets you capture a complex series of actions into a macro script you can run at any time. If you're doing any sort of repetitive work without using an action, you're working too hard.

Unfortunately, most Photoshop users think of the actions capability only in terms of creating prerecorded special-effects tasks. If you examine the actions furnished with Photoshop, you'll find lots of them, including scripts for creating molten lead effects, picture frames, and reflections. Search the Web for "Photoshop actions," and you'll find hundreds of canned macros that create wood grain, wet paint looks, or lightning. They are all great to have because they provide you, in effect, with new Photoshop filters and commands.

However, you can go beyond using actions as special effects tools—way beyond. The projects in this section will show you some ways to think outside the box and use Photoshop's macro capabilities that you probably hadn't considered. All the actions are included on the CD-ROM bundled with this book.

The first project runs you through the basic steps for creating an action, using a very cool lightning effect as its raison d'etre.

64 Create an Action That Applies Lightning to Images

Some great special effects can be created using filters, but you don't want to retrace your steps every time you want to apply an effect. Although manually applying steps isn't exactly reinventing the wheel, it's work you don't have to do if you think ahead and create an *action* first. Follow these steps to prove that not only can lightning strike twice in the same place, it can strike as often as you'd like. This is a variation of a technique you may have seen elsewhere, because lightning effects have become something of an "oldie but goodie," but I've introduced some new tricks in the steps that follow:

1. Choose an image that contains an area you'd like to fill with lightning. Scenic photos with sky often work best, but you can place your lightning effect anywhere you like, in any kind of image.

2. Select the area where the lightning effect will be applied. In this figure, I used the Magic Wand tool to select the sky.

Because the sky already had clouds, I held down the Shift key while clicking in additional areas to add them to the original selection. Then, I used Image➤ Select ➤ Similar to grab all the pixels of a similar tone (particularly the tiny areas between the branches of the trees).

3. Once you've selected the area for the effect, you can create an empty transparent layer (Ctrl/Command+Shift+N), and switch to that so the effect will be applied only to the new layer.

4. Begin recording your macro. First, to make the recording options available, you must turn off Button mode in the Actions palette. (Button mode lets you activate an action by clicking its name button in the palette.) Uncheck Button Mode in the flyout menu at the right side of the Actions palette.

5. Choose New Action from the Actions palette's flyout menu, as shown in the following figure, or press the New Action button at the bottom of the Actions palette (it's to the left of the Trash Can icon).

When the New Action dialog box pops up, you can do the following:

◆ Enter a name for the action that is easy to remember.

◆ Assign the action to the Default set that is loaded each time you launch Photoshop, or assign it to another, more specialized set you have created. (Choose New Set from the flyout menu to create additional sets of actions.)

◆ Bind the action to a shortcut key, such as Ctrl/Command+Shift+F12, so you can activate it at any time by pressing these keys.

◆ Associate a color with the action, making it easier to find in the action Palette when you're using Button mode.

When you click Record, Photoshop will start memorizing any steps you carry out.

6. For our lightning effect, choose Edit ➤ Fill , and select 50% Gray from the Contents drop-down list, select Normal Blending Mode, select 100% Opacity, and make sure Preserve Transparency is unchecked. Click OK to fill the selection with gray.

7. Press **D** to make sure the Photoshop default foreground/background colors of black and white are active.

8. Hold down the Alt/Option key, and then, from the Filter menu, apply the Render ➤ Clouds filter, release the Alt/Option key, and immediately apply Render ➤ Difference Clouds from the Filter menu.

9. Choose Image ➤ Adjust ➤ Auto Levels to accentuate the streaks between the clouds, making them resemble lightning.

10. Choose Image ➤ Adjust ➤ Invert to reverse the selection. Your image should start to look pretty good at this point.

11. Choose Image ➤ Adjust ➤ Hue/Saturation (or press Ctrl/Command+U) to add color to the clouds. Check the Colorize box, then move the Hue slider to a tone you like. (I selected an ominous dark blue, located at the 240 position on the slider.) Then ripen the saturation by moving the Saturation slider over to the 75% position. Click OK to apply the color.

12. Click the Stop Recording button at the bottom of the Actions Palette to finish your macro. Your finished image should look something like this one.

13. To apply the action you've just recorded (or any action), highlight the action in the Actions list and click the Play button; or in Button mode, just click the action's button.

Tips for Fixing an Errant Action

Sometimes your action doesn't perform the way you expected. You can do lots of things to mend your macro, both before the fact (in planning your action) and after the fact (when you have an action that doesn't work correctly):

◆ The most important thing to remember is to record the script while using an image as similar as possible to those you'll be applying the macro to, in terms of size, resolution, and color mode. (That is, don't expect an action recorded with a 300dpi 24-bit color image to operate exactly the same on a 72dpi grayscale image.) Doing so will allow you to see the exact effect you're getting as you record the macro.

◆ After you've created an action, you can edit it by turning off Button mode and clicking the right-pointing triangle (➤) next to the action's name to reveal all its steps. Drag steps you don't want to the Trash Can icon at the bottom of the Actions palette. View the settings that Photoshop used when applying the step, and make sure they are what you want. Click the Record button to start recording additional steps from anywhere in an action.

◆ Before recording the action, bring up the Units And Rulers Preferences dialog box (press Ctrl/Command+K, followed by Ctrl/Command+5), and set your rulers to percentages instead of pixels or some other unit. That will let Photoshop play back any steps that require tracking a relative position in your image accurately.

◆ While you are recording an action, make sure a value in a dialog box is set as you intend (rather than to its current or default value) by changing it to something else and then returning it to the value that appeared when the dialog box first appeared. For example, if you want to set Saturation to 78 percent in the Hue/Saturation dialog box and the value already happens to be 78 percent when the box pops up, change the Saturation to something else, and then *change it back* to 78 percent to make sure the step is captured correctly.

◆ After you've created an action, you can still change the settings in the dialog boxes you worked with when the action was created. For example, perhaps you created an action that uses the Hue/Saturation dialog box to set saturation to –27. Now you decide you want a value of –80 instead. In non-Button mode, list the steps as described in the second bullet point. Double-click the step you want to change. The dialog box will appear, and you can change to the settings you want before closing it.

◆ If you're unsure exactly where a problem lies, use an old computer programmer's trick and play back the macro a step at a time or at reduced speed. You can watch as the action unfolds to pin down precisely where the misstep occurs. Choose Playback Options from the Actions palette, as shown here.

Choose either Step By Step (more of a slow-motion effect, as Photoshop carries out the steps slowly, but doesn't actually stop and wait before continuing) or Pause For __ Seconds, which allows you to insert a genuine pause to let you examine exactly what happened in detail. Return Playback Options to Accelerated (the default mode) when you're finished debugging.

◆ You can also insert a break point that stops an action cold at a particular point. Place the cursor within the action's listing in the Action palette at the point you want to stop the macro. Then choose Insert Stop from the flyout menu. Don't check the Allow Continue button. Your action will stop at this point, allowing you to examine the effects that have been applied so far.

65 Crop Gang Scans

When you have a large number of small things to scan and save, you can take quite a while to scan them one at a time, perform whatever corrections you want to make, and then store them on your hard disk. I run into this situation a lot when I'm scanning items to sell on eBay. I like to be able to scan a bunch of objects at once and then convert them all to individual files of a particular width, for consistency. An action can take all the work out of this chore. Try it the next time you decide to scan your postcard or stamp collection. The following example uses just two objects scanned simultaneously, but the technique works just as well for a dozen or more items. Actually, the more objects you gang together to scan, the more time you save.

Basic Automated Cropping

Here's how I do it. First, here's a basic cropping routine:

1. Group all your objects on the bed of your scanner, and grab a scan of everything on the scanner glass. You'll end up with an image something like the next one.

2. Select the first object to be cropped, using the rectangular Marquee tool.

3. With Button Mode off in the Actions palette, choose New Action from the flyout menu, and enter a name for your macro.

4. Choose Image ≻ Duplicate to create a copy of the scanned image file.

5. Switch back to the original image by clicking it with the pointer. The original selection will still be active.

6. To crop to the selection you made in Step 2, choose Image ≻ Crop.

7. To reduce the size of the image either to a particular percentage or a particular width or height in pixels, choose Image ≻ Image Size from the Menu bar.

8. When the Image Size dialog box appears, type in the number of pixels wide you want the finished image to be, or the number of pixels tall, or the percentage enlargement or reduction you want. I like all of my eBay images to be 500 pixels wide (the height doesn't matter to me), so I entered 500 pixels in the Width area when I created this action. If

you'd rather reduce or enlarge your cropped images (say, to make them 50 percent smaller), you should enter that parameter instead.

9. If the Constrain Proportions box is checked, as the default, the value for the dimension you did not specify is filled in for you automatically. Click OK to apply the resizing.

10. I finished off my macro by choosing Filter ➢ Sharpen to add a little snap to the cropped, resized image.

11. Click the Stop Recording button. Your macro is finished. Because a duplicate of the original is made in Step 4, you have another copy of the scanned image to work with if you want to crop an additional object. Just keep selecting objects and clicking the button assigned to this action to crop as many items from the original scan as you want. When you're done, save the individual files to your hard disk.

NOTE I created several versions of this macro. In addition to the one described here, I made variations that rotate the cropped image clockwise or counterclockwise. That way, the orientation of the item on the scanning bed doesn't matter. When I use this auto-crop feature, I can choose to rotate the final image 90 degrees, if necessary, just by clicking on a different Action button.

Save Your Crops Automatically

The previously described action will leave you with a bunch of open files, all cropped the way you want them, but still waiting to be saved to your hard disk. Of course, you can always save them individually or use Photoshop's Window ➤ Close All (Shift+Ctrl/Command+W) to activate a series of File Save operations. But wouldn't it be nice to have your macro close the files under names you choose after it has finished the other tasks? You can't record Save As operations with custom names, of course. However, Photoshop lets you do the next best thing: you can insert a menu command into an action, and Photoshop will pause while you enter specific information, such as a filename. Here's how to do it:

1. Choose the action you just created in the Actions palette, and click on the last command.

2. Select Insert Menu Item from the Actions palette's flyout menu. This dialog box will appear.

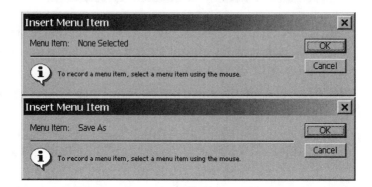

At first glance, it looks like an error message, because it says "Menu Item: None Selected." You might think that you need to select the menu item to insert before choosing this option, but you don't—and you can't, in any case.

3. Choose File ➤ Save As. The name of this command will appear in the dialog box. Click OK to add the menu command to your action.

Thereafter, any time you use this action, the standard Save As dialog box will appear at the end of the macro, allowing you to type a filename for the cropped image. The Insert Menu item command will let you add any menu commands that aren't ordinarily recordable, because they require user interaction when the action is run. I'll show you how to build a palette of commands using this capability in the project that follows.

66 Resurrect the Commands Palette

If you go way back with Photoshop, say to version 3, you probably remember the Commands palette, either fondly or with indifference. Some users found this precursor to the Actions palette supremely useful, while others didn't bother with it. The Commands palette, which is shown here, looked a little like the Actions palette in Button mode, with a series of buttons you could click to activate some of the most common commands.

Commands	
Undo	F1
Cut	F2
Copy	F3
Paste	F4
Hide Brushes	F5
Hide Picker	F6
Show Layers	F7
Show Info	F8
Hide Commands	F9
Fill	⇧F5
Feather	⇧F6
Inverse	⇧F7

The palette could contain only simple commands (including those you added through its customization features), and many of the default choices weren't all that convenient to activate from a Toolbar palette anyway. (Would you rather copy a selection by pressing Ctrl/Command+C, or by moving the mouse over to a palette and clicking on a Copy button?) All in all, the Actions palette, with buttons you could program yourself, was a vast improvement.

However, if you're an old-timer who misses the Commands palette, or you're a newer user who finds the idea intriguing, you can easily embed a reasonable simulation of the Commands palette right within Photoshop's Actions buttons. You can choose the exact commands you want to include, assign them names you find easy to remember, and color-code the buttons to make them easy to find.

The big surprise may be that Photoshop still has a semblance of the original Commands palette included within the Presets ➤ Photoshop Actions folder. It's called Commands.atn, and if you replace the default actions with this set, you'll have a palette that looks like this one.

Actions	
Cut (selection)	F2
Copy (selection)	F3
Paste	F4
Show Color	F6
Show Layers	F7
Show Info	F8
Show Actions	F9
Show Navigator	F10
Image Size	F11
Revert	F12
Crop (selection)	
Flatten Image	Shft+F2
Purge All	Shft+F3
Select Similar (sele...	Shft+F4
Grow (selection)	Shft+F5
Flip Horizontal	Shft+F6
Flip Vertical	Shft+F7
Rotate 90 CW	Shft+F8
Rotate 90 CCW	Shft+F9
Rotate 180	Shft+F10
New Snapshot	Shft+F11
New Snapshot/Cle...	Shft+F12

You'll see that some of the commands are the same as those included on the original palette. There are some new ones, too. You can use this palette as the basis of your own, or you can scrap it and start over with commands that are most useful to you.

To resurrect the Commands palette, just follow these steps:

1. If you want to start with a blank slate, so to speak, remove all your existing actions by choosing Clear All Actions from the Actions palette's flyout menu. You can always append the actions back onto the palette later.

WARNING   If you've already created new actions you want to keep, choose Save Actions from the flyout menu first.

2. Turn off Button mode by unchecking the option in the flyout menu.

3. Choose New Set from the flyout menu. When the New Set dialog box appears, type in a name for your new actions, such as "My Commands."

4. Select New Action from the flyout menu, and enter a name for the action in the New Action dialog box that appears.

5. If you want to color-code your commands, choose a hue from the Color drop-down list. You can also bind the command to a function key, if you like.

6. Click the Record button to begin the command/action.

7. Click Add Menu Item from the Actions palette's flyout menu. Choose commands that you use often, but which don't have shortcut keys associated with them, such as Image ➤ Adjust ➤ Brightness/Contrast.

8. Click the Stop Recording button to add the command to your set.

You can see some examples of the kinds of commands to choose from in the Actions palette.

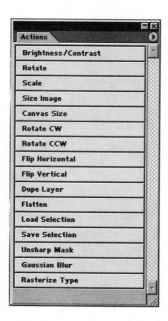

If you color-coded your actions, they can coexist on the Actions palette with other action sets you use.

67 Process a Bunch of Files in One Step

Once you've mastered the actions capabilities of Photoshop 6, you can really save time by processing a whole group of images at one time. You can, for example, convert a whole set of files from RGB color to grayscale in one click or add a white border around cropped images like a picture frame. If you have a digital scanner or camera with an action-compatible "acquire" module (the plug-in software that grabs images from the scanner or camera and imports them into Photoshop), you can perform post-processing on a whole slew of images.

Photoshop's Batch command works on all the files in a single folder, so to perform this magic you'll have to collect all the files into a folder on your hard disk. It's also a good idea to create another folder for Photoshop to deposit the processed files into, so your original images remain untouched.

In all cases, the first step is to create an action that performs the modification you want to make to the file, whether it's converting it from RGB to color, performing an image processing miracle on its contents, or simply cropping it a certain way. You'll find ideas for appropriate actions elsewhere in this chapter.

Change Photoshop Images to PDF Files (Or Any Other Format!)

Adobe Portable Document Format (PDF) files are becoming a medium of exchange between computer platforms and software. Especially if you're working in desktop publishing, you may want to convert a file to PDF so it can be displayed by any software that supports the format—or within Adobe Acrobat or Acrobat Reader. This project shows you how to use Photoshop's Batch command to convert files from one format to another. You can substitute your own file conversion action for the one used here.

WARNING If you create your own file format conversion action, remember to include a Save As command, followed by Close in your original action. The batch process opens files, performs the modifications in the action, and then saves them in their original format. So, you must include a Save As/Close command in the action that will override this.

1. Place all the files to be converted into a folder on your hard disk.

2. Choose File ➤ Automate ➤ Batch to record your batch parameters in the dialog box shown next.

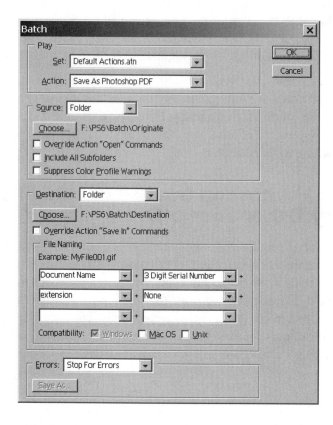

3. In the Play area of the dialog box, choose the Actions set containing the action to be used (in this case, the Default Actions set). Then select the actual action you want to apply to the files.

4. In the Source area, choose Folder from the drop-down list, and then click the Choose button. You can then navigate to the folder containing the files to be converted.

N O T E   You can process files in folders nested beneath the folder you've selected by marking the Include All Subfolders box. If the files are older ones that might have been created using a color profile prior to Photoshop 6, you'll probably want to turn off the color profile warnings.

5. In the Destination area, select Folder from the drop-down list, and click the Choose button to navigate to the folder that is the destination for your modified files.

6. Click the Override Action "Save In" Commands box to allow the action to store the file in the converted format.

7. In the File Naming area, you can specify how the modified files are to be named. You get a great deal of flexibility in choosing the naming style. There are six different drop-down lists, and you can choose a combination of them to ensure that you have a unique filename for each file being processed in the batch:

◆ The Document Name/document name/DOCUMENT NAME options in the drop-down lists insert the current name of the document in initial capped, lowercase, or all-caps styles, respectively.

◆ The 1-Digit, 2-Digit, and 3-Digit Serial Number—as well as Serial Letter (A, B, C) and Serial Letter (a, b, c)—choices will insert consecutively numbered/lettered serial numbers in the filename.

◆ The date choices insert the current day's date in the format you select.

◆ The EXTENSION/extension choices add the file's extension to the filename.

8. Finally, in the Errors area, you can tell Photoshop to stop when it encounters an error (that is, the batch processor is asked to perform an action it cannot carry out) or simply to log the errors to a file you can examine later. You'd want the latter choice if you had a large set of files to process and anticipated only a few errors to deal with later.

Apply Many Actions to Many Files—with One Click!

You may want to use a batch command over and over. Or, you may want to apply several different actions to a group of files consecutively without bothering to create a single action that includes all the modifications you want to make. In either case, your goal is easy to achieve: just record an action that creates and applies several different batch commands—one after the other. Suppose you had an action that reduced an image's dimensions by 50 percent in each direction and another that converted files from RGB to grayscale. Perhaps you had a third action that applied the Canvas Size command to increase the size of an image's canvas by 10 percent, creating a picture frame effect. You can apply all these changes to all the files in a particular folder just by creating an action that includes the appropriate batch commands. Just follow these steps:

1. Create a new action from the Actions palette, and apply a descriptive name.

2. Choose File ➤ Automate ➤ Batch, and create the first batch command.

3. Because you'll be applying successive actions to the same group of files, you won't want to save the modified files in a new location. In the Destination area, choose the same folder as the one that contains the original files. Mark the Override Action "Save In" Commands box.

4. In the File Naming area, make sure only the document name and its extension are used to name the modified files. If you change the filenames by adding serial numbers, you'll end up with multiple files that will, in turn, be processed by the next batch of actions. This figure shows how your Batch dialog box might look.

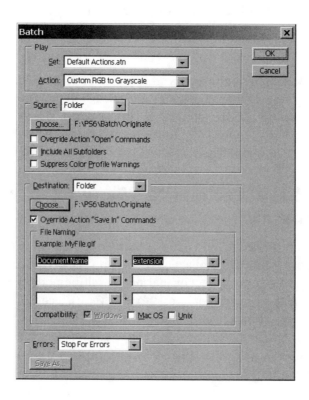

5. Click OK to let the batch run.

6. Repeat Steps 1 through 5 for each of the additional actions you want to apply to the files.

7. Stop recording the batch action. It will appear in your Actions palette as an action you can run at any time.

You'll always have to use the folder specified in the batch action, so remember to clear it out each time you run this action, and then fill it with the next set of files to be processed before running the action again.

68 Apply Actions Outside Photoshop with Drag-and-Droplet

Photoshop 6 introduced a very cool batch-processing mode called *droplets* that lets you transform actions on one or more files (including whole batches) even when Photoshop doesn't happen to be open at the moment. It's more or less a way to save batch operations for reuse, without recording a special action to perform the batch processing.

However, droplets are more powerful in a couple of ways:

◆ You don't have to specify the source folder. Just select the files you want to process and drag them onto the droplet's icon, which can reside in a folder, on your desktop, or on the Windows taskbar.

◆ Photoshop doesn't even need to be loaded to initiate the process. The droplet automatically launches Photoshop and carries out the steps in your action.

To create a droplet, follow these steps:

1. Choose File ➢ Automate ➢ Create Droplet.

2. Click the Choose button in the Save Droplet In area to specify a name and location for the droplet, which is actually a small executable file and will have the .exe extension on the Windows platform.

3. In the Play area, choose the actions set containing the action you want to convert, as well as the actual action to be used as a droplet, as shown here.

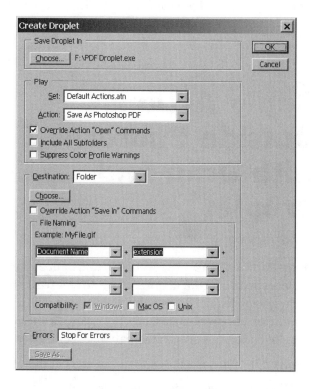

4. You can choose a destination just as you did with batch processes earlier, and you can specify file-naming conventions as before.

5. Click OK to create the droplet.

Thereafter, simply select the files to be processed by the droplet, and drag them to the droplet's icon to apply the action to the entire batch.

69 Create Contact Photo Sheets and Photo Sets

Photoshop's built-in automation tools can streamline some fairly complex tasks for you. There's no need to create an action or set up a special batch of commands. Some useful automated tools are already there for you to use. Two of these are the Contact Sheet capability and the Photo Sets command.

Create Automatic Contact Sheets

The Contact Sheet capability creates a new image with thumbnails of a selection of images you specify. Contact sheets are a great way to preview a group of images without loading each one individually.

Unfortunately, the Contact Sheet command doesn't let you pick and choose which files to include. It operates on every file in a folder/subdirectory you specify (plus any subdirectories below them, if you choose). So, the best way to use it is to copy the files you'd like to include in your contact sheet to their own folder, and then fire away. Here's how to do it:

1. Choose File ➤ Automate ➤ Contact II to produce this dialog box.

Contact Sheet II

- Source Directory
  - Choose... F:\Books\FODDER\Contact\
  - ☑ Include All Subdirectories

- Document
  - Width: 8 inches
  - Height: 10 inches
  - Resolution: 72 pixels/inch
  - Mode: RGB Color

- Thumbnails
  - Place: across first
  - Columns: 5 Width: 0.926 inches
  - Rows: 6 Height: 0.926 inches

- ☑ Use Filename As Caption
  - Font: Arial Font Size: 12 pt

OK Cancel

2. Click the Choose button, and navigate to the folder containing the images you'd like to place on the contact sheet.

3. In the Document area, specify a width, height, resolution, and color mode.

4. In the Thumbnails area, you can control how many images will be included on each contact sheet by entering the number of rows and columns you want. You can also specify the way they are arranged: in rows or columns.

5. If you like, the filename can be used as a caption to help you associate a thumbnail with a particular file. You can choose a font and font size, too.

6. Click OK, and Photoshop will create the contact sheet for you. If all the images won't fit on a single sheet, it will produce enough multiple sheets to hold them all. Several sample sheets are shown here.

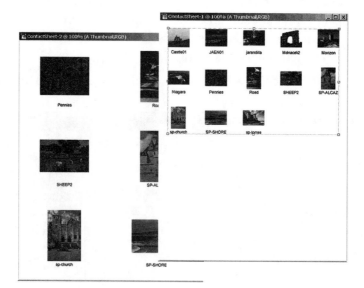

Create Photo Sets

Need to print a 5 by 7 and several wallet-sized photos on a single sheet? Why not? Printing multiple copies of the same picture on one sheet is a great way to save money, especially with photo-quality inkjet paper as expensive as it is. Photoshop can automate this process for you. Just follow these easy steps:

1. Choose File ➤ Automate ➤ Picture Package to produce this dialog box.

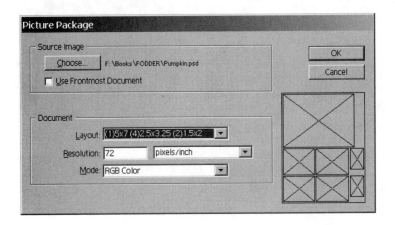

2. Click the Choose button, and navigate to the photo you want to use (or click the Use Frontmost Document button to tell Photoshop to use the topmost image that is already loaded).

3. Select a package format. There are twenty to choose from, ranging from two 5 by 7s on a single 8.5 by 11-inch sheet of paper up through four 4 by 5-inch pictures. There are also many different combinations of picture sizes (including wallet photos). A preview area at the right side of the dialog box shows you the layout.

4. Select a resolution and color mode.

5. Click OK to print a finished picture set like the one shown here.

Photoshop can also automatically create a Web gallery for you, but I'm going to save that for the next part, "Take Your Images to the Web."

Work on the Web

In the past, Photoshop's feature set was criticized for not being Web-friendly. For a while there, Adobe actually expected you to purchase a second, stand-alone application, ImageReady, to handle the most important image/Web functions. Fortunately, this essential tool was folded into the Photoshop package with version 5.5 and, if not tightly integrated with the image editor, ImageReady is at least fairly painless to access as you're working on your Web graphics.

This chapter introduces some of the cool things you didn't know you could do for the Web with Photoshop, with an emphasis on animation. Lots of additional features in Photoshop and ImageReady lend themselves to Web pages, including creating JavaScript rollovers, image slices, and image maps. However, they all involve HTML coding and other concepts that are beyond the scope of this book. Instead, let's jump into some very interesting things you can do with Photoshop and ImageReady in the animation realm. I'll use the projects at hand as an opportunity to explore Photoshop's new custom shape and custom layer styles tools, too.

Admit it. You hate Web pages that greet you with flying ducks, soap bubbles that follow your cursor around the page, blinking text, madly rotating marquees, and other animated nonsense. Nobody cruises the Internet in search of pages that induce vertigo. On the other hand, you've probably welcomed a button that called attention to itself. You admired a logo that seemed to glow with a sparkling sheen. Maybe you even laughed at a well-done cartoon character that graced a particularly attractive Web page.

The difference between dizzying Web graphics and those that use motion effectively is good taste. I can't teach you good taste, but I can show you how to use motion. Photoshop and ImageReady have all the tools you need to create great-looking animated images, using the built-in capabilities of the versatile GIF format. The next few projects show you everything you need to know to get started. I'm counting on you to apply the skills you pick up to benefit humankind and not drive your Web page visitors to distraction. Best of all, you can use these animated GIFs in lots of places other than Web pages, such as in PowerPoint presentations.

70 Animate a Pinwheel

Follow these steps to create your first simple animation:

1. Create a new, transparent document. To make the work a little easier, I created a blank image measuring 600 x 600 pixels. (You'd never use an animation that big on a Web page, of course!)

2. Press **U** to activate Photoshop's line and shape tools in the Tool palette, and choose Custom Shape.

3. Click the Shape drop-down list in the Option bar, and choose Load Shapes from the flyout menu. Select Custom Shapes in the Load dialog box, and click the Load button. Then, select the large pinwheel shape, (it's the second one from the left in the bottom row) as shown below.

4. Drag a pinwheel shape that almost fills your empty image. Hold down the Shift key so the shape will be perfectly symmetrical (which makes it rotate more smoothly).

N O T E Photoshop's Shape tool lets you create any of a set of standard shapes, plus those you create and save yourself, as vector images. As vector graphics, you can edit them, enlarge or reduce them, and perform other manipulations without getting fuzzy edges.

5. The image needs to be centered exactly. The easiest way to do that is to use the Crop tool to trim the image at the edges of the pinwheel. Then use Image ➤ Canvas Size, choose Percent from the drop-down list in the dialog box, and enlarge the document by 110 percent in both height and width.

6. Apply a 3D Layer Style from the Styles palette. Your image will look something like this figure.

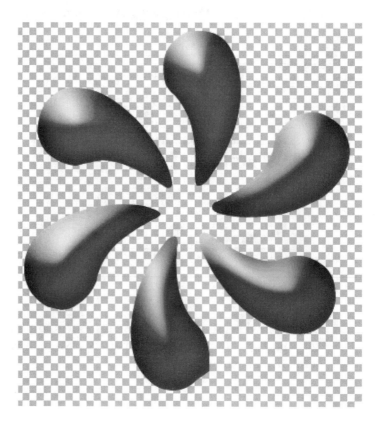

7. Jump to ImageReady by pressing Shift+Ctrl/Command+M.

N O T E   ImageReady and Photoshop share many of the same menus and tools, and you can perform many of the same functions in either application. We are jumping to Image-Ready in Step 7 so that you can get your feet wet if you haven't used it before. In practice, it makes little difference whether you perform the following step or two in Photoshop or ImageReady.

8. Duplicate the layer, and choose Edit ➤ Transform ➤ Rotate 90 degrees CW.

9. Repeat Step 8 twice more. You'll end up with four layers, each rotated 90 degrees from the last.

N O T E   For smoother animation, you can also rotate in smaller than 90-degree increments. Choose Edit ➤ Transform ➤ Rotate, hold down the Shift key, and rotate the image by dragging the handles with the mouse. ImageReady will limit the rotation to 30-degree increments; you could end up with 12 different layers, each offset by 30 degrees from the last.

10. Choose the Animation Palette. From its flyout menu, select Make Frames From Layers. ImageReady will add three frames to the palette's strip, one for each of the other layers.

11. Click the down-pointing arrow beneath each of the frames, and choose a Delay time of .2 seconds. This value determines how quickly the animation will run.

12. Select Forever from the Looping Options drop-down list. You can also specify that the animation will run one-time only or a specified number of times.

13. Watch your animation by clicking the Play button, located just below Frame 3 in the next figure.

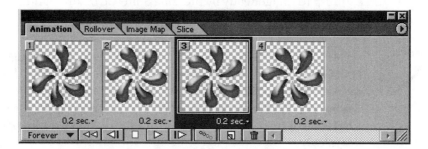

14. Save your animated GIF by pressing Shift+Ctrl/Command+Alt/ Option+S. Give the file a name, and then click Save.

WARNING Because this GIF was created on transparent layers, the animated version will display on a Web page as a transparent GIF. However, if you use any background other than white, you'll notice a fringe around the pinwheel.

71 Tween Your Images

In the last project, you manually created a separate layer for each frame of the simple pinwheel animation. That was good practice, because more complex animations often require creating a series of layers with multiple small manipulations on each. However, for the simplest kind of animated GIFs, you can let ImageReady do all the work of creating the in-between frames using a process called, logically enough, *tweening*. We're going to work entirely within ImageReady for this one, so you can see how its tools mimic those of the main Photoshop application. Follow these steps to learn how:

1. Load the soccer picture shown in the following figure from the CD.

2. Use the Elliptical Marquee tool to copy the soccer ball to a new, transparent layer.

3. On the original background layer, use the Clone Stamp tool to clone grass from the background to fill in the place where the soccer ball remains in the original image. You'll end up with a pair of layers something like this.

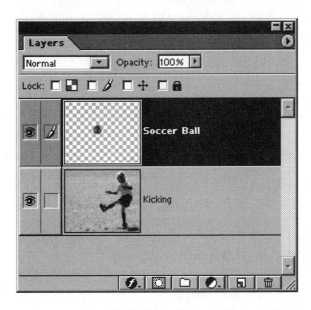

4. With the Animation palette open, highlight the first (only) frame, and choose New Frame from the palette's flyout menu. A second frame, a duplicate of the first, appears. Note that even though both frames appear in the Animation palette as merged images (that is, ball and background together), ImageReady's Layers palette still shows these elements as separate layers.

5. Click the second frame to highlight it. Then click the soccer ball layer in the Layers palette, and drag the soccer ball to the upper-left corner of the layer. The frames in the Animation palette will reflect this modification, and now, as you click either frame, the Layers palette changes to show the relative position of the ball.

6. Click, and Ctrl/Command+click each of the two frames so both are selected, as shown here.

7. Click the Tween button at the bottom of the Animation palette, or choose Tween from the palette's flyout menu. This dialog box appears.

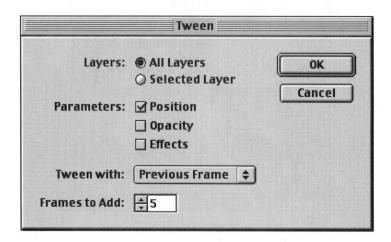

8. Choose from the available options:

Layers You can select to "tween" only one layer (in this case, the soccer ball layer) or all layers in an image. Choose All Layers so the tweened images will contain both the soccer ball and the background.

Parameters Mark the Position check box. This will cause Tween to create between frames, varying the position of the soccer ball starting with the first frame and ending with the last one. You won't need the Opacity box, which varies the transparency of the extra frames to match the values of the first and last frames. You also won't need the Effects box, which blends Layer styles.

Tween With Leave this set at Selection, which tweens between the selected frames.

Frames to Add For this project, choose "5" frames to add to the animation.

9. Click OK to start the tweening process. ImageReady will create a series of frames like the ones shown in the figure that follows.

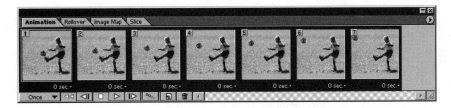

10. Select One Time from the Looping Options drop-down list.

11. Watch your animation by clicking the Play button.

12. Save your animated GIF by pressing Shift+Ctrl/Command+Alt/Option+S. Name the file, and then click Save.

72 Animate Multiple Objects

Animating multiple objects in complex ways can be…complex. I've made this project super-simple so you can see exactly how ImageReady animates multiple layers. Once you grasp the essentials, you'll be able to move on to really complex animations of your own.

1. Open a new, empty transparent document in ImageReady. About 400 x 400 pixels is a good, workable size.

2. Click ImageReady's Type tool, and enter the words **Flying Text** in the upper-left corner, using a typeface and size of your choice (we're just fooling around here, so it doesn't matter).

3. Click the Warp Text button, and choose Arc Lower from the drop-down list.

4. Click the Type tool, and type **Rising Text** near the bottom edge of the document.

5. Click the Type tool, and enter **Falling Text** near the top edge of the document.

6. Choose New Frame from the Animation palette's flyout menu.

7. Select the second frame and move the type contained within the three layers as follows:

   ◆ Move Flying Text to the lower-right corner. Then, choose the Type tool, and change the warp from Arc Lower to Arc in the Options bar.

   ◆ Move Rising Text to the top of the frame.

   ◆ Move Falling Text to the bottom of the frame.

8. Click the Tween button, choose All Layers and Position, and choose "10" frames in the Frames To Add area.

9. Click OK to start the tweening process.

10. Play your animation, and watch in amazement as the type flies around the screen, with the Flying Text type morphing from an upward-curving arc to a downward-curving arc. Pretty easy and pretty amazing, right?

73 Fade to Black... and Back

In our continuing quest to, in Thoreau's words, "Simplify, simplify," this next project will show you yet another piece to the ImageReady animation puzzle. It's an easy one, and not once will you think to ask, "Why didn't Thoreau just say, 'Simplify'?" You'll also get a chance to play with Photoshop 6's capabilities for creating new, custom shapes and Layer styles. Custom shapes and styles are great tools for Web pages because you can create a special look that you can duplicate over and over for additional buttons, rules, or whatever. You can fade your image out, or fade it in, as we'll do in this exercise.

1. In Photoshop, create a new, transparent document.

2. Click the Shape tool in the toolbox, and choose the Rounded Rectangle tool.

3. Draw a rounded rectangle, which will form the foundation of our custom shape.

4. In the Options bar, choose the Oval shape tool and click the Subtract From Shape Area button.

5. Drag in the rounded rectangle shape to remove an oval area from it, producing a new, custom shape that looks like the following figure.

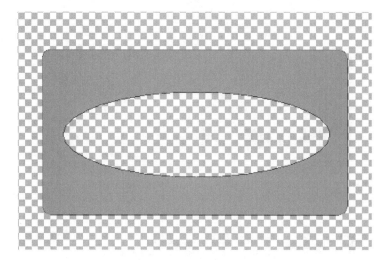

6. Choose Edit ➢ Define Custom Shape, and give your new shape a name.

NOTE Henceforth you can summon this shape from the Custom Shape drop-down list. You can also create custom shapes using the Pen tool or Freehand Pen tool.

7. Choose the Gradient tool from the toolbox. In the Options bar, click the Gradient drop-down list and select Load Gradients from the list's flyout menu. Choose Metals from the Load dialog box, and then click the Load button.

8. Now, create a custom Layer Style. Choose Layer ➤ Layer Style ➤ Gradient Overlay. When the dialog box appears, choose the Brass gradient style from the drop-down Gradient list. Select Linear from the Style List.

9. Next, without closing the Layer Style dialog box, click Bevel and Emboss. Select the Inner Bevel style, the Smooth technique, and a Depth of 100 percent.

10. Click the Texture bar at the left side of the dialog box, and choose the Molecular texture from the Pattern list that appears.

11. Click OK to apply your layer style to the custom shape. The result should look like this:

12. Make sure the Styles palette is visible, and drag the Effects bar from the Layers palette onto the New Style icon at the bottom of the Styles palette (it's between the No Style and Trash Can icons).

13. Enter some text into the center of the button-to-be. Apply a Layer style to the text, if you like. I used Bevel and Emboss.

14. Select the Type Layer, and choose Rasterize ➤ Type. Then, select the custom shape's layer, and choose Rasterize ➤ Shape (or you can select Layer ➤ Rasterize All Layers).You can then press Shift+Ctrl/Command+E to merge the two layers.

15. Press Shift+Ctrl/Command+M to jump to ImageReady.

16. In the Animation palette, choose New Frame from the flyout menu.

17. Select the first frame in the Animation palette. Then switch to the Layers palette, and reduce that frame's Opacity to 0.

18. Click the Tween button, choose All Layers, mark the Opacity box, Tween With Next Frame, and choose to add 10 frames. Then click OK to begin.

19. Your animated GIF will fade in from total transparency. You can adjust the Delay to .01 seconds or more to create a slower fade. Your finished button will look like this (squint your eyes, then open them to visualize the fade-in).

74 Save for the Web

In the bad old days, getting images that were "browser-safe" was difficult. Difficult and thankless because zillions of people were still using monitors that could display no more than 256 colors, and only 216 of them could be safely assumed to be visible in most browsers.

Today, most Web cruisers have computers that show millions of colors, but it's still a good idea to optimize your images so they'll look their best. Photoshop and ImageReady have built-in tools that automate this task for you. ImageReady is especially adept at this task because it simplifies (*simplifies*) looking at an optimized preview before you save. Take the button you created in the last project, and use ImageReady to save it in Web-top shape as a still image. To save it as an animated GIF, jump to the project that follows this one.

1. ImageReady has three preview windows, marked with tabs in the document labeled Optimized, 2-Up, and 4-Up. Click the 2-Up tab for the view shown in this figure.

N O T E The Optimized view shows what your image will look like with ImageReady's default optimization; the 2-Up tab displays your original image at the left or top, with the optimized version at the right or underneath (the layout depends on the orientation of your original image). The 4-Up tab displays your original image and three possible optimization schemes.

2. In the Optimize palette, choose the file format in which you want to save the image. Here, I've selected JPEG High. You can choose the quality level using either the drop-down list or the slider in the Quality area of the dialog box. The higher the quality, the longer it will take to download an image. You can also click the Progressive box to create an interlaced JPEG (which will load alternating lines as it downloads until the full resolution image is visible). Quality settings are:

Low Quality   Any setting from 0 to 29 percent

Medium Quality   Settings from 30 to 59 percent

High Quality   Settings from 60 to 79 percent

Maximum Quality   From 80 to 100 percent

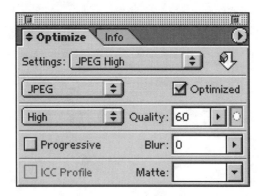

NOTE If you've created a custom set of parameters for a particular file format, you can save those settings for reuse by selecting Save Settings from the Optimize palette's flyout menu. Or, better yet, create a Droplet by clicking the Droplet icon at the upper-right side of the Optimize palette.

3. You can view various tidbits of information about an image in the status bar at the bottom of the document window.

The left-most box contains the current zoom level; you can change the zoom by selecting a new zoom ratio from the drop-down list.

The center box shows the optimized file size and an estimate of how long the file would take to download at 28.8Kbps. You can change this display to any standard download speed for 9.6Kbps to 256Kbps to preview download times for other connections. This center box can also display other information you might want, such as image dimensions or Undo/Redo status, all available from the same drop-down list.

The right-hand box can display any of the same sets of information.

| 100% ▼ | 23K / 9 sec @ 28.8Kbps ▼ | 304K / 23K -- ▼ |

NOTE Choose Optimize To File Size from the Optimize Palette's flyout menu if you have a target size for a file (say, 32K or less) and want ImageReady to apply its optimization settings to achieve that goal.

4. Click the 4-Up button to view several possible optimization scenarios, as shown in this figure.

5. To save an image with a transparent background or as an animation, you'll need to use the GIF format, as shown in the following figure. Choose the number of colors you want to use.

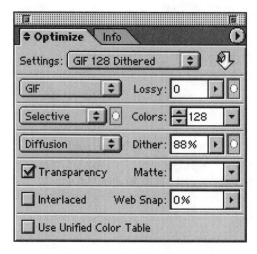

6. Choose File ≻ Save Optimized to save your fine-tuned image.

75 Add Fire to Your Animations

Now is a good time to learn how to make your animations smaller and easier to load. First, I'll have you follow these steps to create that awful flaming logo the guy in the television commercial spends all his time perfecting.

1. In Photoshop, load the Fear file from the CD-ROM. I've already done the hard work of creating it and placing it on a transparent layer. Make sure the Lock Transparency box is not marked.

2. Duplicate the text layer twice.

3. Apply Eye Candy 4000's Fire filter to each text layer in turn. Change the Random Seed and some of the other parameters slightly so each set of flames will be different. The logo will look something like this:

4. Duplicate the background layers, and merge them until you end up with three layers that are identical, except for the flames.

5. Switch to ImageReady.

6. Choose New Frame from the Animation palette's flyout menu. Choose it again to create a total of three frames.

7. Switch to each frame in turn, and make a different layer of the three available visible in each of them.

8. Click the first frame, and then Ctrl/Command+click each of the other two to select them all.

9. Right/Ctrl+click any frame to reveal the Disposal context menu. Make sure Automatic is checked. ImageReady will then look at each frame when saving the animation, and if the following frame contains transparency, it will discard the previous frame to prevent it from "showing through" the next frame.

76 Optimize Your Animation

Because animated GIFs contain so much information, optimizing them so they'll download and display smoothly from the Web is important. Just follow these steps to optimize the flaming text animation.

1. Using the Fear This animation, select Optimize Animation from the Animation palette's flyout menu.

2. Mark the Bounding Box and Redundant Pixel Removal check boxes.

◆ The Bounding Box choice crops each frame so that only the area that has changed from the preceding frame is included. In the case of the current project, the area outside the logo will be excluded.

◆ The Redundant Pixel Removal option changes to transparent all pixels in a frame that are unchanged from the preceding frame. Make sure the Transparency box is checked in the Optimize palette and Frame Disposal has been set to Automatic. Both steps reduce the file size of the animated GIF by eliminating pixels that aren't needed. In this case, everything except the flames themselves and the pixels touched by the flames will be considered redundant and not included in the animation after the first frame.

3. Choose File ➤ Save Optimized to save your optimized animation.

INDEX

Note to the Reader: Throughout this index **boldfaced** page numbers indicate primary discussions of a topic. *Italicized* page numbers indicate illustrations.

What's on the CD?

The CD accompanying this book is packed with stuff to play with—stuff from pictures to plug-ins. The special Sybex Clickme interface is an annotated gateway to everything on the CD-ROM, but here's a brief description of all you get.

Clip Art

A sample gallery of royalty-free Photoshop files, so you can expand on the ideas inspired by each project. Few of these pictures are perfect on their own—all are ready to yield to your retouching and image manipulation skills.

Color Gallery

A high-resolution showcase of the images in the color insert. Not all of the color images are described step-by-step in the text; some of them are "bonus" images that build on the projects included in the book.

Chapter Files

All of the images from the book in full color. I've also included some transitional Photoshop files with multiple layers, so you can see how various images were built.

Software

Try-out software for both the Macintosh and Windows platforms. Thanks to the magic of the CD-ROM file system, you'll see only the software suitable for your particular platform.

Deep Paint (Right Hemisphere Ltd.)   A powerful texturing and painting tool that allows you to brush artistic media—such as oils, watercolors, or crayons—and surface textures—such as scales, metal, or wood—directly onto 3D models (Windows).

Dizzy (Vertigo 3D Software)   Allows you to scale, light, and orient your 3D models for your Illustrator and Photoshop graphics. Includes 500 free models to get you started (Mac).